We Shall Ov~~ercome~~ to
We Shall Overrun

The Collapse of the Civil Rights Movement
and the Black Power Revolt (1962–1968)

Hettie V. Williams

University Press of America,® Inc.
Lanham · Boulder · New York · Toronto · Plymouth, UK

Copyright © 2009 by
University Press of America,® Inc.
4501 Forbes Boulevard
Suite 200
Lanham, Maryland 20706
UPA Acquisitions Department (301) 459-3366

Estover Road
Plymouth PL6 7PY
United Kingdom

Library of Congress Control Number: 2008936444
ISBN-13: 978-0-7618-4353-5 (paperback : alk. paper)
ISBN-10: 0-7618-4353-1 (paperback : alk. paper)
eISBN-13: 978-0-7618-4354-2
eISBN-10: 0-7618-4354-X

™
⊖ The paper used in this publication meets the minimum
requirements of American National Standard for Information
Sciences—Permanence of Paper for Printed Library Materials,
ANSI Z39.48—1984

To my teachers

Francis Dooley, Julius Adekunle, and Brian Greenberg

Table of Contents

Preface

The history of the American Civil Rights Movement has been written largely from the perspective of both social and political history. This work is unique in that it explores the American Civil Rights Movement from the perspective of psycho-intellectual history. Obstacles of strategy and methodology plagued the movement early on and compounding these concerns was the issue of black identity. The intellectual history of African Americans as represented in the diametrically opposing ideas of integration and separation reflects the doubled sense of self awareness in black life and culture. Movement leaders were able to consistently address the concerns of methodology and strategy for the "good of the cause" and yet the debate over 'black power' could not be resolved. The variables of class and gender only compromised further the divisions within the coalition emergent from the 'black power' discussions. Although the history of African Americans includes a vigorous tradition of independent black organization formed out of necessity and in reaction to oppression, the complicated discourse surrounding the black power slogan as associated with black separatism helped to create a break-down in group unity. The history of African American identity politics is the history of African American identity divided against itself.

The traditional history of the American Civil Rights Movement has focused on either national organizations or major personalities. King-centered works by historians such as David Levering Lewis and organization histories by historians such as Clayborne Carson have since shifted to studies of local people. John Dittmer, Adam Fairclough, and Charles Payne have contributed significantly to the development of this shift in focus from the national to the local. The rise of gender studies as an academic discipline has also led to the appearance of scholarship on works concerning pivotal movement women such as Ella Baker, Septima Clark, and Fannie Lou Hamer. Groundbreaking collections of women in the movement include *When and Where I Enter* (1984) by Paula Giddings, *Women in the Civil Rights Movement* (1993) by Vicki Crawford, and *Sisters in the Struggle* (2001) by Bettye Collier-Thomas and V.P. Franklin. Important participant histories in the struggle for black equality from NAACP secretary Walter White's *A Man Called White* (1948) to Roy Wilkin's *Standing Fast* (1982) have served as crucial to the history of the movement. Although recognizing the role of local people within the larger framework of what some historians have identified as the "organizing tradition," this work re-examines the traditional leaders and organizations through a nuanced interpretation.

This book is an attempt to interpret the history of the American Civil Rights Movement through the metaphor of nervous breakdown. Using a topical-chronological approach, focusing on the years 1962 to 1968, this work is a discussion of the movement within the larger historical framework of the African American struggle for freedom. America is the most ethnically diverse country in the world. Major ethnic groups in the United States have routinely used their ethnicity as an agency to secure economic, social, and civil rights.

African Americans have consistently struggled to do the same. Organizations from the Free African Society to the NAACP have worked to secure equal rights. The struggle for black equality became a mass movement in the late 1950s that facilitated the cooperation between the greatest assembly of black leaders and black dominated organizations in American history. As coalition radicals began to chant the slogan 'black power,' they were castigated by the coalition conservatives. These conservatives lamented that the slogan implied an "ethnically tagged" power and openly fretted about white support for the cause. Those who embraced integration exchanged the tradition of self-help and self-reliance for social entitlement embodied in 1960s liberalism. Ethnic groups have historically utilized slogans and created power blocs to secure social reform and political recognition as has been the goal of the African American community until the emergence of 'black power.' This coalition broke down over the meaning, the means, and the attainment of 'black power.' An examination of the five major national groups that made up the coalition for civil rights along with the major leaders associated with these organizations will define this study. How the personality of this group "broke down" is the primary focus of this analysis. Chapter one traces the historical development of modern black nationalism while subsequent chapters discuss the major organizations associated with the coalition for civil rights reform. The concluding chapter addresses the additional factors causal in the collapse of coalition.

Hettie V. Williams

West Long Branch, New Jersey

August, 2006

Acknowledgements

This work would not have been possible without the assistance and guidance of many people. I sincerely acknowledge the help, encouragement and tutelage of my teachers at Monmouth University including Francis Dooley, Brian Greenberg, and Julius Adekunle. The tireless efforts of Mr. Robert Grasso must also be recognized here. It was with the guidance of these teachers at this teaching University that I became a confident student of history. I would also like to acknowledge the support of my family in this endeavor, particularly, my parents Gloria A. Hill and Freddie G. Williams, Sr. and my siblings without their support, guidance, and love I would have never been able to succeed in life.

MAJOR CIVIL RIGHTS ORGANIZATIONS

NAACP   National Association for the Advancement of Colored People formed in 1909 by liberal minded whites and African Americans.

NUL   National Urban League created in 1911 by black reformers as a self-help and public policy agency.

NACW   National Association of Colored Women self-help agency created by black women in the Progressive Era.

NCNW   National Council of Negro Women depression era public policy and self-help agency organized by black women.

UNIA   Universal Negro Improvement Association an international black national-ist organization formed by Jamaican born Marcus Garvey in the 1920s.

NOI   Nation of Islam a black separatist organization created by Elijah Poole in the 1930s.

CORE   Congress of Racial Equality established by seminary students at the University of Chicago in 1941.

SCLC   Southern Christian Leadership Conference formed in 1957 as a result of the Montgomery Bus Boycott.

SNCC   Student Non-Violent Coordinating Committee developed with SCLC's Ella Baker and students involved in the sit-in campaigns of 1960.

COFO   Council of Federated Organizations created by the major civil rights groups in 1962 to coordinate their activities in the Deep South.

LCFO   Lowndes County Freedom Organization independent black political party established in 1964 by Stokely Carmichael in Alabama.

MFDP   Mississippi Freedom Democratic Party independent black political organization developed by Bob Moses in 1964.

BPP   Black Panther Party for "Self-Defense" organized by Huey P. Newton and

Bobby Seale in 1966 first as a black nationalist group.

Us   As in "us" black people united a black cultural nationalist group developed by Ron Karenga in the late 1960s.

RNA   Republic of New Africa black separatist group formed at 1968 conference convened by Milton Henry and his brother Richard.

Introduction

The opposite of all armies, you were best
Opposing uniformity and yourselves;
Prison and personality were your fate.
Yet you who saved neither yourselves nor us
Are equally with those who shed the blood
The heroes of our cause. Your conscience is
What we come back to in the armistice.
Karl Shapiro, "The Conscientious Objector"

The collective *consciousness* of objections to societal norms prompted mass protest in the most turbulent decade in recent American history. Opposing conformity and themselves,[1] with the threat of prison and death as their fate, the 1960s was a decade defined by the continuous ruckus of dissenting groups and individuals. The beatniks, peaceniks, flower children, radical feminists, New Leftists, California lettuce and grape pickers, along with "black power" advocates, were all a part of this combustible patchwork of protest. This climate of dissent had global proportions. While Mao Tse Tung's Red Guards smashed through the streets of Beijing, out of the California ghetto came the Black Panther Party for Self-Defense. As Mexican students clashed with the *granaderos* at the National University, in 1968, French students stomped up the Boulevard St. Michel.

Black radicals closely identified themselves with independence movements in Third World countries. They conceptualized themselves as part of the "colonized" world. The writings of Martinican psychiatrist Frantz Fanon served as a foundation for black power ideologies in the 1960s. Many black radicals also championed the image of the martyred Argentine revolutionary, Che Guevara, who fought alongside Fidel Castro in the Sierra Maestra. The Palestinian struggle against Israel, the Cuban Revolution, and the quest for independence in Africa were all considered viable examples of national liberation. The radicals embraced, alongside Guevara, Ho Chi Minh, Fidel Castro, Mao Tse Tung, and Ghana's Kwame Nkrumah.

The factors of gender, race, class, sexuality, national identity, and geographical location are paramount when considering the 1960s in perspective. The term race in this analysis is used as a social construction not as a biologic category of human difference. The factor of race (as a constructed social reality) can be especially applied to the Black Power revolt of the 1960s. The African American experience is unique within the American experience due to historical circumstance.[2]

The social construction of race as predicated on faulty scientific conclusions about skin complexion and cultural behaviors were used to sustain the slave system. In reaction to the derogation of the black body and oppression, stereotypical images of blackness have been consistently challenged by African Americans. The "other" in America has been determined by appearance, blood, class and sometimes association. Immigrants at the turn of the century, such as those from Southeastern Europe, were able to "negotiate" their ethnicity for "whiteness" according to the white studies scholar Matthew Frye Jacobson in his book *Whiteness of a Different Color*. The degradation of African Americans was justified through stereotypes linked to color and culture. American race science would invariably place African Americans at the bottom of the racial scale based primarily on the condition of color.

The disintegration of the Left, including the collapse of radical feminism, the retreat of black radicalism, and the decline of the New Left, lends itself to a comparative study. The intent of this particular work is not comparative history. This project moves forward *a priori* from the premise that the African American experience is the most "un-American," to use the words of Joanne Grant, of all experiences in America because of the history of *racial* slavery. African Americans have been treated the *most* different due to the construction of race as a social reality used to justify black servitude. Negotiation into "whiteness," whiteness being a fundamental asset of the "fit" American citizen, also according to Jacobson, is ultimately impossible for the African American. Similarities among the dissenting groups must be recognized, but this particular historical analysis is not a comparative one.

The radicalism projected by white college students in the 1960s was similar to black protest, yet it was distinct from the nature of black radical dissent. The French students in Paris, who attacked the archaic French university system, had more in common with white students such as Mark Rudd, at Columbia University, who attacked the traditional structure of the American university system. The radical black cadre that comprised the Student Non-Violent Coordinating Committee (SNCC) and the Congress of Racial Equality (CORE) brought their protest immediately to the society at large. They were far removed from the comforts of campus life in the rural communities of the Deep South. They were not overly concerned with more liberty, as were the students of the Students For A Democratic Society (SDS), but *some* liberty. White leftists, such as the splinter groups of the SDS, could not decide from whence the oppression came or what it was. Was it imperialism, liberalism, or capitalism? A similar ambiguity plagued the Women's Movement. The breakdown of major sects included the politico-feminists who blamed the system of democratic capitalism for the oppression, the liberal feminists who believed it was the lack of employment equity, and the radical-feminists who identified the hierarchical power structure of male dominance for the oppression.[3] The variable of race in fact instigated two movements for women's liberation.

Although black radicals did form alliances with some white radical sects such as the Weatherman, a splinter group of the Revolutionary Youth Movement

and the Peace and Freedom Party, which ran Eldridge Cleaver for President and
Huey P. Newton for California State Assembly, these alliances were separated
by the fact that black radicals had no qualm in identifying the source of oppression, white racism.[4] SDS had an internal conflict in defining "the oppression"
away from the University system after 1964, when the student movement eventually took to the streets.

As SDS moved toward building an interracial alliance among the poor and
working class through 1965, with the establishment of their Economic Recovery
Action Projects in northern cities, the students of SNCC were in retreat from the
ideology of integration.[5] While both segments of the student movement held a
disdain for organizational structure, institutional authority, and were outspoken
opponents of the war in Vietnam, the issue of race was understood as an important factor of difference.[6] Virtually ousted from the ranks of the black liberation
movement, Abbie Hoffman understood that his movement was a different one,
"Black Power to me, as a young white radical, has no real meaning. The question should be directed to blacks. I am busy making my own revolution. I am
busy building a new community."[7] The radicals in SNCC and CORE were in
retreat from liberalism *and* the ideology of integration. The pre-conditions of the
Black Revolution, based upon the emphasis of black self-identity and self de-
terminism, were set by the Student Nonviolent Coordinating Committee and the
Congress of Racial Equality, in the Deep South, as they broke away from the
national vanguard for civil rights reform.

Martin Luther King, Jr. was at the center of this break. The conservative alliance between the National Association for the Advancement of Colored People
(NAACP) and the National Urban League (NUL) stood firmly against "black
power." The rationale behind this project is to demonstrate how the competing
forms of Black Power ideologies emerged and destroyed the greatest consensus
of black leadership. This national coalition for civil rights, formed between the
Southern Christian Leadership Conference, the Student Nonviolent Coordinating
Committee, the Congress of Racial Equality, the National Association for the
Advancement of Colored People, and the National Urban League, garnered the
greatest achievements in civil rights legislation for African Americans since the
period of Radical Reconstruction. The ideological conflicts over the meaning,
the means, and the attainment of "black power" split this coalition in half.

This "crisis" of both individual and group identity has been a force that has
repeatedly promoted and ultimately compounded continuous disunity within the
black community as a whole. The lack of a unified body of ideas concerning
"black power," as a slogan and concept, failed to crystallize in the 1960s because there was no unified sense of self for the African American. Therefore, we
can look at the split as a microcosm of a larger disunity existent within black
America. The continuous crisis of identity in the black community was ultimately responsible for the final collapse. One must also recognize that super-
imposed over the impediments of strategy and methodology in African American protest thought there are profound issues of identity. This crisis of identity
will be discussed as an *identity psychosis*.[8]

A distorted sense of self, or identity psychosis, was most prevalent in the black community before and during the collapse of the coalition. The binary nature of black protest thought has been influenced by *both* a positive and negative, or distorted, sense of self that many African Americans experience on a daily basis. The separatist rationale was that black people would have to become white, sacrificing their black identity, in order to ever achieve integration. Separatism became aligned with the positives of blackness, while integration was associated as a negative response to the goal of "black power."[9] The nature of black protest thought reflects this distorted sense of self. This analysis, therefore, has to move beyond questions of strategy and methodology in black protest thought.

The split between black leaders and black dominated organizations within the Civil Rights Movement, characterized as a nervous breakdown, provides a nuanced interpretation of the collapse of this coalition. This project is an attempt to describe the complexities of the collapse of coalition by illustrating the ideological divide within the group as a breakdown of personality. One must also be careful *not* to infer that the whole of the black community suffers from a pathological mental disorder. On the contrary, it is a testament to the triumph of the human spirit that African Americans have survived the unmitigated "psychological trauma" of "living in a white supremacist society and being the constant targets of racist assault and abuse."[10] The metaphor of nervous breakdown is utilized to *illustrate* the psychological implications of a doubled sense of self-awareness in America that African Americans must endure.

The false perceptions of the black African as a sub-human beast of burden were used to justify slavery. Through the history of slavery *and* emancipation, these perceptions became, to the slave master and his descendants, a *reality*. The dominant preconceived "reality" of the African American as somehow less than human forced the descendants of slaves to live within a distorted reality, a lie. Harold Cruse has stated that, because African Americans exist under "the dominating persuasion of the Great American Ideal," the nationalist elements of black protest thought have been denied the dignity of acceptance as "an ethnic conception of reality."[11] Ralph Ellison's invisible protagonist succinctly described his inadequate existence:

> I am invisible, understand, simply because people refuse to see me. . . . You often doubt if you really exist. You wonder whether you aren't simply a phantom in other people's minds. . . . You ache with the need to convince yourself that you do exist in the real world, that you're a part of all the sound and anguish, and you strike out with your fists, you curse and you swear to make them recognize you. And, alas, it's seldom successful.[12]

Nikki Giovanni addresses this theme of invisibility in a recent poem:

> you know something is very wrong that no one listens to you no one ever knows you are standing there talking . . . no one pays any attention to you and

you are asking for is a chance to present your side of the question it's like you understand that you just don't matter.[13]

African Americans seem to fade in and out of their American existence quite often.

The reality forged and maintained by the dominant culture has created for the African American a disjointed American personality: one black and one American. Most black people in America have both a positive [American] and negative [black] sense of self that sometimes attempts to co-exist. Two bodies *will never* occupy the same space at the same time. The word *nigger* has both positive and negative connotations. The term "nigga," within the black community, has become a part of the communal voice as, sometimes, a term of endearment and brotherhood. This crisis of the African American has become a crisis of human identity and human existence brought on by "living within a lie."[14] The dominant social reality in America is based upon the derogation of black and the veneration of white. This has created, for the African American, a distorted sense of self. This distorted sense of self has led to a pattern of disorganized thinking about blackness. According to Vaclav Havel, writing as a Czech dissident, living within a lie can lead to "existential schizophrenia."

African American writer James Baldwin, in a talk with a group of New York City public school teachers in 1963, made some assertions on the notion of schizophrenia in black America:

> any Negro who is born in this country and undergoes the American educational system runs the risk of becoming schizophrenic. On the one hand he is born in the shadow of the stars and stripes and he is assured it represents a nation which has never lost a war. He pledges allegiance to that flag which guarantees "liberty and justice for all." He is part of a country in which anyone can become President, and so forth. But on the other hand he is also assured by his country and his countrymen that he has never contributed anything to civilization, that his past is nothing more than a record of humiliations gladly endured. He is assured by the republic that he, his father, his mother, and his ancestors were happy, shiftless, watermelon-eating darkies who loved Mr. Charlie and Miss Ann, that the value he has as a black man is proven by one thing only-his devotion to white people.[15]

In the process of building the intellect, through the American educational system, also according to Baldwin, the African American child learns "the shape of oppression."[16]

The existential dilemma of the African American resonates within the writings of Baldwin. In his book *The Fire Next Time* Baldwin writes to his nephew and namesake James, "I am writing this letter to you, to try to tell you something about how to handle *them*, most of them do not yet really know that you exist." He goes on to state that, African Americans are "taught really to despise themselves from the moment their eyes open upon the world," and that the "universe has evolved no terms" for a black existence in America-none but those determined by white society.[17]

This notion of "existential schizophrenia" has become a major theme of black intellectual thought today. The Harvard scholar Cornel West has defined the problem of black identity as "existential angst." It is the contention of West that this angst, or sense of worthlessness and self-loathing among Black Americans, "resembles a kind of collective clinical depression" derived from "the lived experience of ontological wounds and emotional scars inflicted by white supremacist beliefs and images."[18] Derrick Bell, a former professor of law at Harvard University, has suggested that the level of self rejection and self destruction among black people in the inner city today is derived from a despair of self. Many African Americans, in fact, seek refuge in this "self-rejection" according to Bell.[19]

Black and white Americans, in fact, share the *same* reality, according to Baldwin—an American reality. This reality is a reality that has been historically informed by a white supremacist belief system. Most blacks are of two mindsets; retaining emotional ties to an almost mystical African past, while intellectually realizing that they are Americans too.[20] According to Baldwin, in his book *Notes of a Native Son*, every image about blacks is indeed controlled and preconditioned by this reality imbued with negative caricatures of African Americans. Therefore, there can be no black reality without the pervasive influence of whites. Black Power? There *can be* no such thing.

The moderates within the coalition were intensely concerned with what white people would think about the provocative phrase "black power." There are some excruciating, and disturbing, psychological implications surrounding the nature of black protest thought in America. Because the black and the white both *depend* on the same reality, it is the contention of Baldwin that "any new society is impossible to conceive."[21] Everything thought about "black" is already preconditioned and ultimately controlled, in one way or another, by the dominant reality. Marcus Garvey was promptly deported as soon as *his* black nationalist movement gained mass appeal. Segregation, or black separatism *defined* by white people, flourished while Garvey was removed. Baldwin's basic premise is that, what black people think, if it is to have any legitimacy, *must* be heavily conditioned by *what white people think is best.* This is a story about power and control.

According to the African American psychiatrist Alvin Poussaint, the influx of a white presence in the Deep South, during the Mississippi Summer project of 1964, had a debilitating effect on the black volunteers within the movement.[22] The presence of whites in the movement became an important point of contention for the lead articulators of "black power." The rationale behind the exclusion of whites from the SNCC, delivered in 1966, was psychological. Whites were to be excluded because of their "intimidating effect" on black people, and because their presence had the power to "change the complexion of the meeting" of any given group of black people.[23] This pattern of disorganized thinking about "black" became a part of the fostering of black protest thought revolving around the issues of separation and integration. The value of black has been historically measured by white preconceptions of African Americans. It became such that, from the debate among black Abolitionists, through the Du Bois-Washington debates, to Marcus Garvey and beyond, separation was seen as a necessity or prerequisite to self-actualization. The separatists believed it was deemed impossible for African Americans to develop a true sense of self within a white reality. The integrationists advocated inclusion into the American system which they saw as essentially egalitarian. The separatist viewpoint was based upon the belief that blacks simply could not attain any real power in white America. Blacks could not assimilate because the ideal American personality is white and not black. Many separatists saw complete integration into American society as implausible. To the black separatist, integration was seen only as a prerequisite to assimilation on white terms.

It was CORE's James Farmer who asserted that the debate over desegregation became imperceptibly "shaded into a demand for black dispersal and assimilation." Farmer also went on to assert that, "We were told, and for a while told ourselves, all Negro separation was inherently inferior, and some of us began to think that Negroes couldn't be fully human in the presence of other Negroes."[24] This pattern of thinking about "black-separatism" began to infect the consensus for coalition. Black power was labeled "separatism," while integration began to take on the veneer of accommodation. James Farmer recognized that in order for black people to fully assimilate, they would have to give up their very identity and undergo a process of "self denial and self abasement."[25]

Notes

1 Feminists opposed one another, as did the advocates of "black power," and those involved in the American Indian Movement, and the New Left-all opposed society and "themselves" at the same time.

2 The Middle Passage and Ellis Island are not remotely comparable analogies. The passage of the "new immigrants," of the turn of the century, to assimilation has occurred, with only transitory episodes of isolation and discrimination. The experience from slavery to freedom, as blacks migrated to the cities of the north, has been marred by the permanence of homogenous racial isolation, rather than transitory enclaves. The ghetto became a permanent feature of black residential life through the 1930s. One could easily make the assertion that the black ghetto is simply an urban analogue of the reservation or plantation.

3 Alice Echols, *Daring to be bad: Radical Feminism in America: 1967-1975* (Minneapolis: University of Minnesota Press, 1989), 33. The Women's Movement, with its juxtaposed purpose of equality through gender neutrality and gender difference, can be more closely correlated to the Black Power revolt.

4 SNCC does begin as a college movement, but almost immediately removes itself from campus life away from the mainstream of society. At SNCC's founding conference there were students both black and white. Tom and Casey Hayden join SNCC in the Deep South as well, along with such organizations as the National Students Association, and the United States Student Organization-among other groups. Tom Hayden was nearly bludgeoned to death in Mississippi for "freedom riding." But it was not until after 1964, that SDS gains a significant presence away from campus life through the ERAP program.

5 In 1966, whites are expelled from the civil rights movement by the Student Nonviolent Coordinating Committee and urged to go organize "their own communities."

6 An examination of the comments made by Carl Davidson, Tom Hayden, Andrew Kopkind, and Greg Calvert, in such journals as *New Left Notes, Studies on the Left,* and *Liberation* suggest that the New Left recognized the core of difference that separated the student movement from the black liberation movement between the years of 1967 and 1969. Greg Calvert asserted that white students should "organize around their own oppression." Carl Davidson insisted that, "organizing struggles over dormitory rules seemed frivolous when compared to ghetto rebellions" and that white students were "no longer wanted nor necessary in the black movement."

7 Abbie Hoffman, "Black Power: A Discussion," *Partisan Review* 35 (Spring 1968): 208.

8 According to the *Mosby Medical Encyclopedia*, a psychosis is medically defined as any major mental disorder, with an emotional or physical source, in which the personality may not be able to function smoothly and may be characterized by severe depres-

sion; also, the personality is characterized by a pattern of disorganized thinking. **Functional psychosis** is defined by personality changes and the loss of the ability to function in reality. For the purpose of this research the term *identity psychosis* has been newly formulated.

9 To many separatists, the goal of integration for black people was implausible, because Americans were integrated by race-not class, culture, or religion; the common denominator amongst the white majority was race.

10 Bell Hooks, *Killing Rage: Ending Racism* (New York: Henry Holt & Company, 1995), 134.

11 Harold Cruse, *The Crisis of the Negro Intellectual* (New York: William Morrow & Company, 1967), 6.

12 Ralph Ellison, *Invisible Man* (1947; New York: Vintage International, 1980), 3-4.

13 Nikki Giovanni, "This Poem Hates," in *Blues For All The Changes* (New York, 1999), 20-21.

14 Vaclav Havel, "The Power of the Powerless," in *Open Letters: Selected Writings, 1965-1990*, edited by Paul Wilson, 125-215 (1985; New York: Vintage Books, 1992). Havel's greengrocer lives within the lie of the *post-totalitarian* Communist state in Czechoslovakia; according to Havel, living within a lie produces a "profound crisis of human identity."

15 James Baldwin, "The Negro Child-His Self Image," remarks delivered to 200 New York City teachers at one of their professional in-service meetings on October 16, 1963, published in the *Saturday Review*, December 21, 1963.

16 Ibid.

17 James Baldwin, *The Fire Next Time* (New York: The Dial Press, 1963), 6, 25-30.

18 Cornel West, *Race Matters* (New York: Vintage Books, 1993), 27.

19 Derrick Bell, *Faces At The Bottom Of The Well: The Permanence of Racism* (New York: Basic Books-Harper Collins, 1992), 4.

20 The term schizophrenia is derived from the Greek meaning for "two-minds." Schizophrenia is medically defined as one form of psychosis.

21 James Baldwin, *Notes of A Native Son* (1955; Boston: Beacon Press, 1984), 21.

22 Alvin Poussaint, "How the 'White Problem' Spawned Black Power," Ebony August, 1967, 89.

23 SNCC, "Position Paper on Black Power," in *Modern Black Nationalism: From Garvey to Louis Farrakhan*, ed. by William L. Van Deburg, (New York: New York University Press, 1997), 120.

24 James Turner, "The Sociology of Black Nationalism," *The Black Scholar*, (December, 1969): 25.

25 Ibid.

Chapter 1

Black Power?

*The effective range of this special power
cannot be measured...*
Vaclav Havel, "The Power of the Powerless"

Chief Justice Roger B. Taney of the United States Supreme Court enunciated these notions [first as Attorney General under Andrew Jackson] in his opinion on the Dred Scott decision in 1857:

> The African race in the United States even when free, are everywhere a degraded class, and exercise no political influence. They are not looked upon as citizens by the contracting parties who formed the Constitution. They were evidently not supposed to be included by the term citizens . . . they were at the time considered as a subordinate and inferior class of beings, who had been subjugated by the dominant race and whether emancipated or not . . . had no rights or privileges.[1]

Before and after the American Civil War, with the decision in the Dred Scott case in 1857, and later with the *Plessy v. Ferguson* decision in 1896, the African American was dehumanized in society and law[2] The psychological indoctrination used to sustain the slave system was based upon the myth of white racial superiority and the perceived inferiority of the black African. This idea became the dominant social reality for the majority of Americans. This mythological perception remained the accepted *given* reality with the end of slavery. The dominant social reality of the majority has had an alienating affect on African Americans. Tunde Adeleke has stated that, "The traumatic and dehumanizing experience of slavery, even with the denial and negation of the history, culture, and nationality of blacks, failed to completely "denationalize" the consciousness of blacks. The more blacks were demeaned and alienated, the stronger their national "consciousness grew."[3] There is a distinct historical development behind the psychological implications of the split as nervous breakdown. Slavery was a system of social control sustained through psychological terror enhanced through physical torture. The control simply did not end with slavery nor did the terror. African Americans, out of their unique historical circumstance in America, managed to develop a "vision of nationality." There emerged a vigorous national consciousness within this pattern of "disorganized thinking." Thinking became "disorganized," by the 1960s, because many moderate African Americans began to view all forms of black separatism as inferior or backward. They essentially denied their own particular ethnic group an "ethnic conception of

reality" with their denunciation of the separatist impulse. This pattern of "negative thinking about black," on the part of the integrationists, illustrates this idea
of distorted thinking.

Stereotypical images of African Americans are well documented in American history. The supposed innate inferiority of the African American, in dra-
matic or comic entertainment, in literature, commercial advertisement, and film
was continually emphasized. Through nearly 100 years of American film, images of the degradation of blacks, based heavily upon physical appearance, have
appeared in the form of blackface, the blacker faces of the subservient Tom, the
bafoonish coon, the "tragic mulatto", the garish Mammy, and "Farina" the
pickaninny.[4] Sociologist Alphonso Pinkney has stated that because blacks are
the most "racially distinct from the predominant Northern European ideal," they
have in many ways been subjected to the greatest abuse.[5] Stereotypes are what
justify and sustain patterns of prejudice and discrimination.

The trauma of wanting in, while remaining out, has created within black
America an identity psychosis that affects the group as well as the individual in
the group. It can be likened to a form of "existential schizophrenia" that plagues
the group, and the individual within the group, in detrimental and debilitating
ways.[6] This is not to say that the average African American, because of racial
oppression, suffers from a crippling mental disorder, but *it is* to say that their
black identity is in a constant state of turmoil. This daily assault on the African
American sense of self has a history. A constantly shifting self creates a dilemma of self-awareness that could potentially lead to self-destruction or nervous break-down. They are black and they are American. Their human identity
has been constantly challenged because of the dominant Euro-American culture
that has consistently devalued black culture the black self. Black people in
America are in a constant flux of crisis regarding their American personality.

W.E.B. Du Bois recognized the symptoms of identity psychosis early on:

> It is a peculiar sensation, this double-consciousness, this sense of always look-
> ing at one's self through the eyes of others, of measuring one's soul by the tape
> of a world that looks on in amused contempt and pity. One ever feels his twon-
> ess,—an American, a Negro; two souls, two thoughts, two un-reconciled striv-
> ings; two warring ideals in one dark body, whose dogged strength alone keeps
> it from being torn asunder.[7]

These "two souls," "two thoughts," "two-un-reconciled" strivings and "two war-
ring ideals," are classic symptoms of existential schizophrenia. A brief overview
of the manifestation of *identity psychosis*, used as a tool to illustrate the psychological dimensions of the debate over power within the black community, from
Douglass to Garvey and beyond, should lead to a discussion of the distinct categorical features of the Black Power revolt that emerged leading to the breakdown of the coalition.

"Most black people are schizophrenic," stated the self-styled black nationalists Frederic Gaddis.[8] This eternal conflict of the African American has been well illustrated in black literature and black culture. The theme of *identity psychosis* manifested itself most profoundly in black literature. The poets of the Harlem Renaissance to the present were cognizant of a sense of "two-ness." Many prominent African American writers such as Richard Wright, Langston Hughes, and Toni Morrison have explored the theme of the divided self in their writings as well.

The Harlem Renaissance poet Claude McKay insisted that the speaker in one of his poems was a "dark soul" trapped within a "white city."[9] The McKay poems are particularly worthy of note here regarding the theme of identity crisis. In his poem "Enslaved" McKay tells us, "my race has no home on earth," and in his poem "The Negro's Tragedy" McKay relates that his true identity, his true self, is hidden in a "shroud of night which hides and buries him from other men."[10] In the poem "I Know My Soul," also by Mckay, the speaker contemplates that, "I see a part and not the whole," but is comforted by the fact that "I Know My Soul"—a soul that goes unseen.[11] Countee Cullen's poem "Heritage" also embodied this internal conflict. In this poem, Cullen's Africa is described as "one three centuries removed" and as "a book one thumbs listlessly through." The poet is clearly torn between two worlds and two identities as he ponders "the lie;" in "Heritage," the artist has yet to come to terms with his distorted existence, "With my mouth thus, in my heart,/Do I play a double part."[12] The poet Langston Hughes described the African American experience as the "American Heartbreak/Rock on which freedom stumps its toe."[13] Hughes, like Cullen, illustrated the mystical connection to Africa in his poem "Afro-American Fragment" by describing Africa as an "atavistic land" whose "dark face" was far away, and yet eternally connected to his American reality, but he is an "Afro-American Fragment."[14]

Ralph Ellison and Toni Morrison eloquently portrayed the affects of "existential schizophrenia" on the African American personality in their writings as well. The nameless protagonist in Ellison's *Invisible Man* simply withdraws from society, into invisibility. The young character in Morrison's tale simply yearns for the *Bluest Eye*. Toni Morrison's Sethe, the main character in her novel *Beloved*, carries the psychological, and physical, scars of her identity upon her back, in the form of a tree.[15] Richard Wright's Bigger, the protagonist in his novel *Native Son*, finds himself embroiled within a "white world" not unlike the dark soul in McKay's poem "The White City."

> The snow had stopped falling and the city, white, still was a vast stretch of roof—tops and sky. He had been thinking about it for hours here in the dark and now there it was, all white, still. But what he had thought about it had made it real with a reality it did not have now in the daylight. When lying in the dark thinking of it, it seemed to have something which left it when it was looked at. Why should not this cold white world rise up as a beautiful dream in which he could walk and be at home, in which it would be easy to tell what to do and what not to do?[16]

Bigger was never "at home" in the strange white world that would not accept his blackness—he a native son. Due to the weight of the strain, he eventually suffers a Breakdown—this is the symbolism of Bigger's insanity.

The angry words of James Baldwin, one of the most prominent and prolific writers of modern America, rattled off the page and signified *identity psychosis.* In his book *Notes of a Native Son,* Baldwin described being black in America as a "bastard of the West," and the African American as made by God but not in His image. He also spoke of despising his blackness, because they [black people] "failed to produce Rembrandt."[17] In order to have any existence, Baldwin contemplated that he would have to "appropriate" the images of white people and make them his own.[18]

The existential dilemma can also be found in black music and the day-to-day debates concerning African American custom. In these forms, the dilemma boarders on self-denial/self-destruction and, at times, becomes completely nihilistic. The melodies of black America are [and were] about hopelessness, fear, and ultimately about the threat of nothinglessness—redemption found only in death. Da Lench Mob "can't cope with a blue eyed Jesus," as Tupac Shakur ponders in "I Wonder if Heaven got a Ghetto?" *I wonder if Heaven got a ghetto?* There is no hope, even in death, "if heaven got a ghetto." Because of lived experience, the message in the Negro Spiritual and Gangsta Rap seem to be the same. As many slaves made their way to the Door of No Return on the Isle of Goree, many hurled themselves off cliffs. On their way to the Americas, they committed suicide and infanticide. Death was the final act of defiance. Tupac Shakur's song "Nothing to Lose," and the old Negro Spiritual "I Believe I'll Go back Home," carry a nihilistic motif. The slaves pondered that their freedom would be secured in death. A disturbing corollary can be found between the Negro spiritual and Gangsta rap.

The contemporary debate over such everyday rituals as black hair care reflects this identity crisis as some African American contest the practice of pressed, permed or dyed hair, while others venerate the practice of braided or natural hair. The discussion over ebonics, or "black English," and the process of skin bleaching are also serious debates within the black community reflective of this identity psychosis. This identity crisis has also been a feature of black intellectual and political life. It was most apparent in the debate over the meaning, the means, and the attainment of "black power" in the 1960s. This debilitating psychosis permeated the consensus for coalition in the struggle for civil rights. Amid the backdrop of urban riots, the crisis in leadership became a crisis in community as well. The split in the vanguard has to be looked upon as a manifestation of the continuous "symptoms" of an identity crisis that continues to be a debilitating factor in the black community today. In 1966, the civil rights vanguard suffered a nervous breakdown or simply a split personality disorder. The persistent barrier of "split personality" within black protest thought has been a serious impediment to cohesive and consistent black leadership from Booker T. Washington to Martin Luther King, Jr. and beyond. Martin Luther King, Jr., through the Southern Christian Leadership Conference, was at the center of the "break" in 1966, while the SNCC-CORE collaboration battled the NAACP-NUL alliance for the ideological hegemony of the movement.

The psychological analogy of "nervous break-down" is a unique illustration through which to understand the inner dynamics of the split in the civil rights coalition that involved the National Association for the Advancement of Colored People, the National Urban League, the Student Nonviolent Coordinating Committee, the Congress of Racial Equality and the Southern Christian Leadership Conference. This kind of continuous disunity within the black community, or symptoms of *identity psychosis*, is a major impediment to black empowerment in whatever form it may take cultural, political, or economic. Black political and economic power in America demands coalition. If unity among black leaders continues to crumble, or simply break-down, a debilitating erosion of political and economic power will remain. The historical unfolding of the debate over power and the categorical features of the break will define the collapse as nervous breakdown, while the evolution of individual personalities, and the ideological justifications for or against "black power," will demonstrate the integral dynamics of the split.

The internal conflict of wanting in and wanting out, while still remaining "out," was a distinct feature of black Abolitionism through 1860, evident in the dissension between Booker T. Washington and W.E.B. Du Bois between the years of 1895 and 1915, and was a major concern of Marcus Garvey and his heirs through the American Civil Rights Movement. Some, but not all, black Abolitionists supported the migration of American blacks back to Africa. Many prominent white Americans such as Henry Clay and Bushrod Washington, through the institution of the American Colonization Society formed in 1816, favored this notion as well. But before the American Colonization Society endorsed and financed the West African Colony of Liberia for free slaves, which became an independent country in 1848, Paul Cuffee settled some thirty blacks in Sierra Leone in 1815.[19] Although the repatriation of American blacks to Africa became a solution to get rid of an impending racial problem for many white Americans, it became a serious question of debate for some black Abolitionists who saw it as a viable plan for survival. The separatist impulse in black America became a serious part of the discussion amongst the organized community of black Abolitionists that developed between the years 1830 to 1860. This was the era of the National Black Conventions.

The black Abolitionists who opposed Frederick Douglass, the most prominent black leader of the period, created the foundation for black nationalist thought in America. Some advocated for the migration of American blacks to Canada, South America, Haiti, and Africa. Bishop James T. Holly, the first black Anglican priest, supported black migration to Canada then Haiti where he eventually emigrated to in 1861. Edward Blyden and the Episcopalian priest Alexander Crummell wrote and spoke extensively on the subject of trial seperation. Crummell recognized the problem of black identity in America early on, "Because exaggerated contempt has been poured upon us, we too become apt pupils in the school of scorn and contumely. Because repudiation of the black man has been for centuries the wont of civilized nations black men themselves get shame at their origin and shrink from the terms which indicate it."[20] Blyden saw the return to Africa as a means to black economic and political regeneration while Crummell believed that blacks were "destined" for a return to Africa; it was to be a return home.[21]

The most important figures of the immediate decades following the Civil War were Martin Robison Delany (1812-1885), Frederick Douglass (1817-1895), and Henry McNeal Turner (1834-1915). The physician, politician, newspaper editor, explorer, and soldier Martin Delany, who also served briefly as a co-editor of the *North Star*, was a contemporary adversary of Douglass. While Douglass was convinced that he was not only a citizen by "birth and lineage," and that he would therefore advocate for the Negro "his most full and complete adoption into the great national family of America," it was Delany who compiled the first comprehensive literary justification for black emigration in his 1852 text *The Condition Elevation and Destiny of the Colored People of the United States*. Martin Delany actively pursued his theory of repatriation of blacks to Africa. In 1859, he visited West Africa, signed treaties with King Docemo of Logos and Alake of Abeokuta, in the hope of securing a place for black resettlement.[22] Although the Douglass approach to black equality primarily prevailed in this period, there was a significant level of dissent. One of these dissenters was Bishop Henry McNeal Turner author of the "black to Africa" movement at the turn of the century. It was Bishop Turner who first suggested that perhaps God was black. He also called for the formation of a black militia to stave off attacks from the Klu Klux Klan. If Douglass was convinced that he belonged in America, Delany, Turner, and others literally pulled the other way. They followed the path of territorial separatism as developed within a Pan-Africanist framework. Martin Delany developed the ideological basis for modern black nationalism. This foundation was enhanced by Bishop Turner and utilized by Marcus Garvey in the 1920s.Marcus Garvey came to Harlem in 1918, shortly after the death of Bishop Turner in 1915. Turner had been one of the major critics of Booker T. Washington, who became the most influential black leader in America upon the death of Frederick Douglass in 1895. Adjacent to the agitations of Henry McNeal Turner, at the turn of the century, there was the Washington-Du Bois debate.

The views of Frederick Douglass prevailed, although un-realized, until his death in 1895. That same year, Booker T. Washington made his infamous "Atlanta Compromise." Washington was the most important African American spokesman from 1895 until his death in 1915. Born a mulatto slave in 1856 Virginia, Washington was emancipated at the age of nine and went to work in the salt furnaces and coal mines of Malden, West Virginia. He managed to earn an education through the help of the Freedmen's Bureau, pulled himself *Up From Slavery*, and eventually founded the Tuskegee Normal and Industrial Institute in 1881. Washington's reign was not without conflict. Washington received voracious criticism from the black intellectual community.[23]

William Monroe Trotter attacked Washington in his Boston *Guardian* established in 1901. Trotter was one of the most outspoken opponents of Washington's philosophy of accommodation and compromise. Although there were many others, Booker T. Washington's most staunch nemesis was William Edward Burkhardt Du Bois. Born in Great Barrington, Massachusetts in 1868, Du Bois was educated at Fisk and Harvard. He became a historian and sociologist who challenged the core of Washington's belief in accommodation.

Washington's leadership paralleled the emergence of the black intelligentsia. Du Bois was the most prominent black intellectual of his day. He helped to form the American Negro Academy in 1897. And in 1899, he compiled the first sociological text on black Americans ever to be published entitled *The Philadelphia Negro*. The first major black novelist Charles Chesnutt, author of such books as *The Conjure Woman* and *The Marrow of Tradition*, and the first major black poet, Paul Laurence Dunbar, were contemporaries of Washington and Du Bois.

Booker T. Washington and W.E.B. Du Bois were contemporary adversaries. With attitudes shaped by experience and background, both Washington and Du Bois came to certain conclusions about the black race in America. The debate ensued because Du Bois came to view Washington's theory of social conciliation to segregation, along with his emphasis upon vocational education, as demeaning and ultimately detrimental to the race. The argument between Booker T. Washington and W.E.B. Du Bois was about power—black power.

Washington unveiled his thoughts in what has come to be known as the "Atlanta Compromise. This address was given at the opening ceremonies of the Atlanta Exposition of 1895. He received a serious critique of his ideas from W.E.B. Du Bois in Du Bois's 1903 book entitled *The Souls of Black Folk*. In his address, Washington cautioned that material wealth and economic stability should precede social justice and political power. For him, black power was economic power achieved through the "thrift" of manual labor, industry, and entrepreneurial endeavor. Washington seemed to "compromise," for black Americans, social justice and political power, for the obtainment of material progress and economic gain. Washington insisted that his people should "cast down their buckets where they are," and *could* remain "as separate as the fingers" in the process toward economic stability. Although Washington cautioned voluntary separatism, in the quest for economic power, he does not substitute material wealth for social equanimity which he saw as "privileges to come." Washington was a political conservative who reasoned that "no race is long ostracized" if they can move with caution.[24] Accommodation through black self-reliance was a means to an end for Washington. For him, the meaning of black power was to be found in material wealth that would eventually lead to economic stability, social justice, and political power.

According to W.E.B. Du Bois, there was no need for compromise nor accommodation. Du Bois bargained on the "extremist folly," agitated for immediate unrestricted political rights, and argued for comprehensive social justice. He was an elitist, and academic, who envisioned a meritocracy or rule of the "Talented Tenth" to guide the black masses. Du Bois thought Washington's emphasis on industrial education mediocre and disdainful, but what rankled Du Bois the most was Washington's theory of submission or accommodation. He specifically criticized, in his book *The Souls of Black Folk*, Washington's idea of accommodation as demeaning and his emphasis on industrial education as "narrow minded." Du Bois believed that African Americans could not freely accumulate a vast amount of material wealth without the full benefits of American citizenry. He was convinced that economic stability could not be gained, maintained, or sustained, by black Americans without the ballot:

> Is it possible, and probable, that nine millions of men can make effective progress in economic lines if they are deprived of political rights, made a servile caste, and allowed only the most meager chance for developing their exceptional men? If history and reason give any answer to these questions, it is an emphatic *No*.[25]

It was important to Du Bois not to separate the pursuit and maintenance of material wealth from the attainment of political power and social equanimity. He believed that political power and social power was inextricably linked to economic power. He criticizes Washington on these points. While Booker T. Washington became the national spokesmen for the race, Du Bois remained an ardent supporter of black civil rights.

Du Bois was also concerned with the problem of black identity and the hope of inclusion into American society for the African American. Du Bois thought it questionable as to the notion that the African American would be able to "merge" his "double self:"

> In this merging he wishes neither of the other selves to be lost. He would not Africanize America, for America has too much to teach the world and Africa. He would not bleach his Negro soul in a flood of white Americanism, for the world. He simply wishes to make it possible for a man to be both a Negro and an American, without being cursed and spit upon by his fellows, without having the doors of opportunity closed roughly in his face.[26]

Because Du Bois found it ever difficult to merge his Negro/American self into one complete ideal, he gravitated toward an increasingly radical stance. The idea of the 'divided self' in black America has a long history.

Du Bois, along with a group of other black intellectuals, organized the Niagara Movement in 1905 and called for "full manhood" suffrage and an end to segregation. This movement eventually led to the formation of the National Association for the Advancement of Colored People in 1909. With the establishment of a Legal Defense Fund, the NAACP waged an assault on segregation. The campaign waged by the NAACP battled such issues as equal access to the ballot, wage differentials, and residential segregation. Counsel for the NAACP a argued and won such cases as *Gunn v. United States* in 1915 that declared the "grandfather clause" unconstitutional, the *Nixon v. Herndon* case of 1927 which eliminated a Texas law that barred blacks from voting in the "white primary," and in 1936 it won the decision in *Gibbs v. Board of Education* which was the first in a series of cases against the practice of public school segregation.

Although Booker T. Washington and W.E.B. Du Bois were, outwardly, philosophical adversaries, both seemed to have lived their lives in great contradiction to the espoused beliefs. Washington publicly cautioned accommodation, but orchestrated a private war against segregation, as his biographers attest:

> Washington turned to secret methods to undermine the system of racial discrimination that he publicly acquiesced in, and at the same time he launched underground attacks on his black critics. In the deepest secrecy, he raised funds, hired lawyers, and directed the strategy of test cases against the Louisiana and Alabama grandfather clauses, against racial discrimination on the Jim Crow railroad cars, against the exclusion of blacks from juries when black criminal defendants were on trial, and against the widespread southern practice of peonage, or debt slavery . . . he kept his part in court cases a secret except to a handful of confidants.[27]

Booker T. Washington lived a double life. If we consider that Washington made his "compromise" during the greatest period of extralegal violence against African Americans across the American south, within the period of the "terrible 90s," one has to infer that for Washington outward conciliation was the best way to survive.

Du Bois, once a staunch supporter of integration, became an outspoken critic of the practice as outlined by the strategies of the NACCP. In the 1920s he moved toward developing a synthesis of Pan-Africanism, while having previously been a critic of Marcus Garvey. Between the years of 1934 and 1948, Du Bois moved in and out of sync with the goals of the NAACP. In the 1950s, he became an ardent advocate of world peace, and nuclear disarmament, as Chairman of the Peace Information Center which was labeled "communist" by some leading U.S. officials. By the time of his death in 1963, W.E.B. Du Bois had renounced his American citizenship and relocated to the newly independent West African nation of Ghana. He died in self-imposed exile—a voluntary separatist. His American personality was never completely whole but rather "torn asunder." The same can be said for Booker T. Washington in his public persona for accommodation and his private war against segregation.

With the death of Booker T. Washington in 1915, the black protest movement moved North along with the masses of some 4 million African American migrants between the years of 1910 and 1940. The movement moved North to Harlem. Born in St. Ann's Bay Jamaica in 1887, Marcus Aurileus Garvey came North too. Marcus Garvey corresponded with Booker T. Washington before he came to Harlem in 1918 to establish the New York branch of his Universal Negro Improvement Association. When he arrived, he was subsequently likened to a garish fool by W.E.B. Du Bois. Marcus Garvey was the father of modern Black Nationalism. Garvey's movement was the first mass African American nationalist movement. Within less than ten years time, Garvey had established more than 700 chapters of his organization in the United States and more than

200 abroad with chapters in more than 40 countries.[28]

Through the guise of the UNIA, Garvey managed to establish three news-papers, including the *Negro World* in New York and the *Blackman* in Jamaica, the Black Star Shipping Line and the Negro Factories Corporation that employed several in the New York area. The Garvey organization was also responsible for creating a host of other businesses such as restaurants, laundries, and hotels. The cornerstone of Garveyism was race pride, economic nationalism, and territorial separatism. Garvey highly emphasized black self-reliance.

Marcus Garvey's movement had experienced mass growth by 1925, and influenced the creation of rival organizations. But that same year, Garvey was convicted of fraud, and for suspicious business dealings, and was given a five year prison sentence. He served two years of this sentence, and was eventually released in 1927. He was immediately deported. One of the groups that the Garvey movement influenced was an organization created by W.D. Fard in 1933 Detroit. Although the Nation of Islam can be looked upon as the most legitimate heirs to Marcus Garvey, the influence of Garvey permeates modern black nationalist thought. Garvey's African centered universe [Garvey saw Africa as the "father of civilization" and continuously venerated black culture] became the cornerstone of cultural nationalism, and later Afrocentrism. There are shades of Garvey's thoughts that can be linked to Ron Karenga's *Kawaida*, Swahili for what is customary and traditional, theory as promulgated through his Us organization in the 1960s.

The cultural nationalism of the 1960s takes root in the Harlem Renaissance during Garvey's era. Garvey's *Negro World* was a primary developer of the concept of the "new negro." This involved the admiration of black identity and pride in everything African. Garvey insisted that black history enabled African Americans to stand "top most among other men," and that Africa was great because "all other continents copied their civilizations from Africa."[29] Garvey saw a black national entity in Africa as a necessity, and made it the foremost objective of the UNIA because it was for "the protection" of the race. Garvey saw that the black race would never be free and always remain "at the mercy of other people" if territorial integrity was not secured.[30]

All of Garvey's heirs, as did the detractors and competitors to Garveyism, wanted power, Black Power. But the question would arise, what is Black Power? It means many different things to different groups and individuals within the black community. Martin Luther King, Jr. contemplated that Black Power had different and congruent meanings:

> Since Black Power means different things to different people and indeed, being essentially an emotional concept, can mean different things to the same person on differing occasions; it is impossible to attribute its ultimate meaning to any single individual or organization. One must look beyond personal styles, verbal flourishes and the hysteria of the mass media to assess its values, its assets and liabilities honestly.[31]

To the National Association for the Advancement of Colored People (NAACP), it meant gradual assimilation into the existing system through legal methods. The National Urban League (NUL), formed in 1911 as a social service agency, concerned itself primarily with the conditions of black Americans in urban areas. Its goals were similar to those of the NAACP. A new methodology formed in the 1940s with the activism of the Congress of Racial Equality, established in 1942, and the individual activism of individuals such as Asa Philip Randolph and Bayard Rustin. Randolph was chiefly concerned with employment equity. For him, black power was to be found in the work place through unionism. The socialist activist Bayard Rustin, a veteran activist of the "new" methodology, was instrumental in creating the Southern Christian Leadership Conference in 1957.

All major segments of the black community agree that there must be power for the black American, but a conflict of meaning and method has created communal competition as it did in 1966. The split in the vanguard for civil rights, if accurately viewed, has to be looked upon as a "breakdown" of leadership and community. The fundamental duality of circumstance, regarding black identity, has shaped ideological competition and fostered disunity. This fundamental duality has been a threat to, and within, the black community disturbing its very fabric at all levels. It has created, at times, within the black community, an anomic atmosphere, one that is socially unstable, alienated, and disorganized from the generalized American personality. The categorical features of the debate shifted and expanded, from integration and separation, to include pluralism and experimentalism in the 1960s.

If we are to look at the split as a microcosm of the *identity psychosis* which plagues the entire community, the classical paradigm for a revolution can be used as a blueprint to describe the categorical features of the debate over "black power." There is no single generic definition of the term "black power." This is due to the fact that "black power" had a series of concurrent and corresponding definitions. "The term Black Power has a range of related but distinct meanings. Because of this it is impossible to find any one summary definition that encapsulates the essence of the movement as a whole," states political scientist John T. McCartney in his book *Black Power Ideologies*. The categorical features of the black power revolt away from coalition attest to this notion of a "range of related but distinct" meanings. The most practical terms that best describe the split to form the *Black Power* paradigm are (a) integration, (b) separatism, (c) pluralism, and (d) experimentalism. To understand the inner dynamics of the breakup, these terms must be first defined then applied.

Integration

The adherents of integration believed in the American system of democracy which they saw as basically humane and equalitarian. They believed in the American dream. The debate over "black power" engaged some of the staunchest defenders of integration such as Roy Wilkins of the NAACP, Whitney Young of the NUL, A. Philip Randolph, and Bayard Rustin. They can be described as the "true believers" of the Civil Rights revolution. The American dream was attainable for American blacks according to the integrationist mindset. To them America was, ultimately, a homogeneous society of integrated groups. African Americans could obtain power through the democratic process and the free enterprise system within the parameters of the law. The integrationists believed that through the methods of non-violent direct action, legal challenge, and legislative measure, black empowerment could be secured. Black power was to be found by utilizing and becoming part of the system. The integrationist mindset will be explored in Chapter Two.

Separatism

The separatists harbored an unflinching hatred against the dominant Euro-American value system, and described it as morally corrupt, evil, and inept. They saw "the system" as deeply embedded with, indestructible, institutionalized white racism. Only through some form of separation could "black power" and an appropriate black identity be attained and maintained. Black power separatists used the means of independent black organization towards the end of some form of separation, either culturally, economically, or territorially. Not all black nationalists were headed to Africa. The Pan-Africanist framework of Delany and Garvey was largely abandoned by the 1960s. Black national consciousness has taken many forms. Under the umbrella of separatists, we can include territorial nationalists, economic nationalists, and cultural nationalists. Using his *Kawaida* theory, cultural nationalist Ron Karenga saw black culture, based in African tradition, as the primary vehicle to black liberation.[32] The quest for a separate African centered [Afrocentrism] identity was the primary goal of the cultural nationalists. To the cultural nationalist, integration was seen as a denunciation of black culture, and a capitulation to white culture and authority. An illustration of the separatist impulse will be discussed in Chapter Three.

Pluralism

The Black Power pluralists tended to view America as a heterogeneous amalgamation of competing cultures, special interests groups, and power blocs. For them, America was composed of a plurality of competing ethnic groups *all simultaneously* vying for power. Pluralists placed a great emphasis on their particular ethnic group and were primarily concerned with improving the power of their personal community. The majority of pluralists sought adaptation to the American system by creating parallel political structures or implementing independent black businesses through free enterprise. The means of independent black organization would lead to the end of Black Power, which they saw as adapting through to the system. While many pluralists such as Charles V. Hamilton viewed complete integration as ultimately implausible and impractical, some used the means of independent black organization towards the achievement of integration. The lead articulators of 'black power' in the coalition were members of CORE and SNCC such as Stokely Carmichael, Floyd McKissick and Jim Forman. The pluralist approach to power, developed by SNCC and CORE in the Deep South, will be studied in Chapter Four.

Experimentalism

Although a vague term, the phrase experimentalist, or experimentalism, for the purposes of this study, will be used to describe the revolutionary black nationalists and black socialists. This was a group that was greatly dissatisfied with the American system and sought a radical alteration to it. They believed white racism fundamentally flawed the system. Therefore, without radical change, the system was irrevocably damaged. Operating from a nationalist framework, in an anti-imperialist context, the experimenters were willing to adjust their doctrines for the good of change, as long as the system changed for the betterment of black society. They sought to alter and not completely destroy the system. Never rigidly doctrinaire, the experimentalists were willing to "experiment" with almost any liberating ideology including socialism. Under this heading, we can include such movements as the Black Panther Party and the Republic of New Africa, as well as individuals such as Robert F. Williams, and Malcolm X. The experimenters will be detailed in Chapter Five.

The *Black Power paradigm* is a shifting paradigm. Also, when we consider the term *nationalism*, as it applies to this study, black nationalists generally identified with *one* or more of the following goals: a distinct separate culture base (cultural nationalism), economic control of personal community (economic nationalism), or the goal of territorial integrity (territorial nationalism). The Black Power paradigm shifted significantly during the collapse of the civil rights coalition in 1966. It shifted to encompass the political pluralists and the experimenters. The emergence of a new black consciousness, contained in the pluralist and the experimental approach to power, *in fact* worked to facilitate the break as the movement for civil reform morphed into the struggle for black identity. The aforementioned categories will define the progression of this study, as coupled with the extended metaphor of the split as a nervous breakdown. This book flows from a topical approach. The break-up of group unity will be handled as if it were a split in personality and discussed under the aforementioned categories of black power ideologies. This study is an attempt to illustrate, through history, the broad psychological implications of the split in black protest thought through the guise of comparison [group unity as *compared* to the split in an individual personality] and metaphor. The integrationist approach to power will be discussed first in the next chapter.

Notes

1 Roger B. Taney, "Opinion of the Attorney General," and "Opinion of the Court in Dred Scott," in *Dred Scott v. Sanford: A Brief History with Documents*, ed. Paul Finkelman, (Boston: Bedford Books, 1997), 56-58.

2 The unanimous decision in the *Brown* case of 1954 that "separate was inherently unequal" does connote a change in public opinion, ushered in by years of activism and protest.

3 Tunde Adeleke, *Un-African Americans: Nineteenth-Century Black Nationalists and the Civilizing* Mission (Lexington: University Press of Kentucky, 1998), 31.

4 Donald Bogle, *Toms, Coons, Mulattoes, Mammies, and Bucks: An Interpretive History of Blacks in American Films* (New York: Continuum, 1994), 6.

5 Alphonso Pinkney, "The Assimilation of Afro Americans," *The Black Scholar,* (December 1969): 36.

6 The former Czech dissident, now president of the Czech Republic, Vaclav Havel spoke of the theme of existential schizophrenia in his essay "Second Wind." "The theme of human identity and existential schizophrenia was everywhere-but now, it all seemed to take place on a completely different level: the time of oral juggling was over and it became increasingly obvious that human existence was at stake."

7 W.E.B. Du Bois, *The Souls of Black Folk* (1903; New York: Signet Classics, 1982), 45.

8 Frederic Gaddis, Personal interview. 30 Nov. 1998.

9 Claude McKay, "The White City," in *The Black Poets*, ed. Dudley Randall, (New York: Bantam Books, 1971), 61.

10 Ibid.

11 Ibid.

12 Countee Cullen, "Heritage," in *The Black Poets,* ed. Dudley Randall, (New York: Bantam Books, 1971), 97.

13 Langston Hughes, *Selected Poems of Langston Hughes* (1959; New York: Vintage Books, 1990), 9.

14 Ibid.

15 Morrison uses the analogy of the ghost of Beloved, a representation of the ghost of slavery, to illustrate the fact that the African American identity remains to be impaired *because* of slavery; this effects the descendants of slaves and slave masters. The African American *human identity* has yet to be emancipated from the justification of the slave system which rested upon the notion of the sub-human character of the black African.

16 Richard Wright, *Native Son* (1940; New York: Basic Books, 1989), 226.

17 James Baldwin, *Notes of a Native Son* (1955; Boston: Beacon Press, 1983), 7.

18 Ibid.

19 John T. McCartney, *Black Power Ideologies: An Essay in African-American Political Thought* (Philadelphia: Temple University Press, 1992), 16.

20 Alexander Crummell, "The Relations and Duties of Free Colored Men in America to Africa," *African American Perspectives: Pamphlets from the Daniel A.P. Murray Collection, 1818-1907*, found at www.memory.loc.gov/cgi-bin/query/r?ammem/murray

21 McCartney, 21-25.

22 Tolagbe Ogunleye, "Dr. Martin Robison Delany, 19th Century Africana Womanist: Reflections on His Avant-Garde Politics Concerning Gender, Colorism, and Nation Building," *Journal of Black Studies* 28, (May 1998): 628-650.

23 The National Negro Committee, in 1910, criticized Washington for giving a "false impression of the Negro." Many other prominent blacks of the day such as Charles Chesnutt and Bishop Henry McNeal Turner also criticized Washington.

24 Booker T. Washington, *Up From Slavery* (1901; New York: Penguin Books, 1986), 223-224.

25 W. E. B. Du Bois, *The Souls of Black Folk* (1903; New York: Signet Classics, 1982), 88.

26 Ibid.

27 Louis R. Harlan, "Introduction," in *Up From Slavery*, by Booker T. Washington (1901; New York: Penguin Books, 1986), xvii.

28 Edward G. Rogoff, "Perhaps the Times Have not Yet Caught up To Marcus Garvey, An Early Champion of Ethnic Entrepreneurship," *Journal of Small Business Management* 36 (July 1998): 66-72.

29 Marcus Garvey, "African Fundamentalism: Fount of Inspiration," in *Marcus Garvey Life and Lessons*, ed. Robert A. Hill and Barbara Bair, (Berkeley: University of California Press, 1987), 15.

30 Marcus Garvey, "Aims and Objects of the U.N.I.A.," in Marcus *Garvey Life and Lessons,* 15-17.

31 Martin Luther King, Jr., "Where Do We Go From Here," in *.A Testament of Hope: The Essential Writings and Speeches of Martin Luther King, Jr.,* ed. James Washington, (New York, 1986), 575.

32 Scot Ngozi-Brown, "The Us Organization, Maulana Karenga, And Conflict With The Black Panther Party: A Critique of Sectarian Influences on Historical Discourse." *Journal of Black Studies* 28 (November 1997): 157-172.

Chapter 2

The
Ceremony of Innocence

The ceremony of innocence is drowned… while the worst
Are full of passionate intensity.
William Butler Yeats, "The Second Coming"

The greatest coalition for the advance of civil rights within black America, that crossed generational and ideological boundaries, eventually collapsed under the weight of the strain. Martin Luther King, Jr., who was at the center of it all, could not maintain it. He was at the center of the revolution because that is where his trusted colleagues in SCLC, and the media,[1] placed him. The ceremony of innocence, as exemplified through non-violent direct action, was everywhere drowned in the blood of countless comrades. Although the modern Civil Rights Movement began with the groundwork of the NAACP, the complete organizational framework must include the National Urban League, along with CORE, SCLC and SNCC.

The "black power" stance embraced by some in the coalition forced the vanguard to move away from coalition into ideological schism, with the NAACP and NUL pitted against SNCC and CORE. Martin Luther King, Jr., through SCLC, made a valiant attempt to maintain the balance. He was criticized on both sides. William Butler Yeats tells us when, "Things fall apart, the center cannot hold." King's movement shifted out from under him, and expanded, moving from a largely rural base in the Deep South, to the urban centers of the North. Before 1966, the movement seemed to pursue King's leadership, but after 1966 it was surely King who followed the movement. The problem of black inequality was much larger than King envisaged.

While King's leadership extended the movement in many circumstances, his stature was connected to a network of other organizational ties deeply rooted before December 1955.[2] The King persona greatly dwarfed others within the movement, with a base of support that included his personal advisors, legal counsel, and speech writers. The socialist-activist Bayard Rustin and the New York lawyer Stanley Levinson were both instrumental in the original concept of SCLC; forces from the northern "old left", and the traditionalism embodied within the southern black Church, formed key influences upon King and his mission.[3] The King biographer Stephen B. Oates has argued that King was in fact "chosen" to lead the Montgomery movement because he personified both of these elements within his character.[4] His trusted aide Ralph Abernathy, himself an important black leader in Montgomery, lacked the middle class polish of King, and E.D. Nixon[5] lacked the educational background.

According to Adam Fairclough, the greatest weakness of SCLC as an organization was that "it could not formulate a separate identity from King the individual and its very structure appeared to be built around him."[6] The formation of this organization was built upon the oratorical ability and the appeal of King at Montgomery, but it was the NAACP lawyers who argued the constitutionality of the city's segregation policy. The structure of SCLC, centered about King, generated conflict with parallel organizations with dissimilar structures. It was only inevitable that King's campaign in Montgomery would merge with that of the NAACP, the NUL, and CORE. A majority of the insurgent local black leadership that comprised SCLC were formerly members of the NAACP, as were many of the students who came to form SNCC in 1960 with the encouragement of SCLC. Although King remained an inspiration to SNCC, his philosophy of non-violent resistance existed primarily as an initial organizing theory rather than a model kept in complete practice.

With the advent of the King leadership in 1957, Roy Wilkins of the NAACP and Whitney Young of the NUL saw their leadership eclipsed by the charismatic leader from Montgomery. In retrospect, the superimposed image of King [the martyr] over the entire movement has virtually diminished thorough discussions of their important roles in the coalition. Roy Wilkins had occupied a position with the NAACP for nearly thirty years by the 1960s. He had become one of the most powerful black leaders in America alongside labor leader A. Philip Randolph before the King ascendance. The goal of complete integration, through government action, had become the ingrained program of the NAACP as articulated by the National Secretary Roy Wilkins. Whitney Young held similar objectives for his organization. Along with Martin Luther King, Jr., A. Philip Randolph, and Bayard Rustin, the Black Power integrationists included Roy Wilkins and Whitney Young.

This chapter specifically concerns King's interpretation of Black Power and the moderate response to Black Power. King viewed the movement in deep philosophical terms, as opposed to the practical persuasion of Whitney Young, or the pragmatic legalisms of Roy Wilkins. King saw the quest for integration as an ethical dilemma. His interpretation of Black Power was basically one of acquiescence.

King's position on Black Power matured from 1962 to 1966, as the struggle in the Deep South progressed. The James Meredith March Against Fear in 1966 forced King to make a choice.[7] It was in 1962 in Albany, Georgia that King met his most cunning foe in the form of Albany Police Chief Laurie Prichett, and the barely constrained animosity of SNCC, many of whom were veterans of the Freedom Rides the previous spring. At Albany, during a movement instigated by the activism of SNCC's Charles Sherrod and Cordell Reagan, King's presence briefly invigorated, but then abruptly deflated the campaign to desegregate the small Southwest Georgia city. The movement resulted in the arrest of many individuals but without achieving any substantive civil rights achievements. After a year of struggle, Albany, Georgia remained segregated. This was the coalition's first major setback. As the jails filled, they were emptied by Police Chief Prichett and the movement stumbled.

Through March and April of 1963, King and the coalition ran into Birmingham City Public Safety Commissioner Eugene T. "Bull" Conner. It was at Birmingham that King wrote his now historic essay on the vindication of civil disobedience entitled "Letter From a Birmingham City Jail." The Birmingham campaign led to serious concessions to implement plans for desegregation by the fall. This campaign also led to the March on Washington in August 1963. One month after the March On Washington, King returned to Birmingham to give the eulogy for four little girls who had their small bodies incinerated in a terrorist bombing at the 16th street Baptist Church. Medger Evers, an NAACP activist from Mississippi, was murdered on his doorstep two months before the coalition went to Washington.

King's travels through Birmingham led him to Selma, Alabama in 1965. The planned journey from Selma, Alabama to the State capital in Montgomery, held by a contingent of civil rights activists, was halted by what has become known as "Bloody Sunday" on March 7, 1965. SNCC, smarting from the defeat at the 1964 Democratic National Convention, and incensed at the injury of their Chairman John Lewis, wanted to continue the march immediately without a court order. King insisted on a court order and the march did not continue for several days until one was granted. Many in SNCC chose to abandon the continuation of the March altogether. If the events at Selma signified a fragile stand for the coalition, the events at Greenwood, Mississippi in 1966 during the James Meredith March Against Fear signified the coalition's last stand.

King's ideas about "black power" were developed, and enhanced, during the continuation of the Meredith March in 1966. This was a march that, disturbed by its implications, Roy Wilkins and Whitney Young chose to abandon.[8] King initially interpreted the use of the term by black activists as incendiary,[9] or simply a bad choice of words. He made an attempt to appease the radicals with the suggestion of the term "black consciousness," as the March progressed:

> I conceded the fact that we must have slogans. But why have one that would confuse our allies, isolate the Negro community and give many prejudiced whites, who might otherwise be ashamed of their anti-Negro feeling, a ready excuse for self-justification? "Why not use the slogan 'black consciousness' or 'black equality'?" I suggested. "These phrases would be less vulnerable and would more accurately describe what we are about. The words 'black' and 'power' together give the impression that we are talking about black domination rather than black equality.[10]

On June 15, 1966, after the Greenwood incident, in which Stokely Carmichael popularized the phrase "black power," King moved closer to the radical position.

Martin Luther King, Jr. made "black consciousness" the focal point of his last convention[11] as President of the Southern Christian Leadership Conference. He eventually came to the conclusion that Black Power was not only a call to black consciousness, but also the possible pooling of black economic and political resources. King also saw "black power" as a bid for psychological emancipation. In the months leading up to his assassination, between the summer of 1966 and the spring of 1968, King stated that black people needed to "discover how to organize our strength in terms of economic and political power."[12] He also went on to state that, "Power is not the white man's birthright; it will not be legislated for us and delivered in neat government packages. It is a social force any group can utilize by accumulating its elements in a planned, deliberate campaign to organize it under its own control."[13] King began to more fully embrace, and indeed defend, the pluralist approach to power, "the nettlesome task of Negroes today is to discover how to organize our strength into compelling power so that the government cannot elude our demands."[14] In his last book *Where Do We Go From Here: Chaos or Community?* published in 1967, King discussed the pluralist approach to power. He described it as the pooling of black financial and economic resources, and believed it to be the most "positive" meaning of "black power."[15]

Martin Luther King, Jr. only repeated this theme in his "I See the Promised Land" sermon on April 3, 1968 given at the Bishop Charles Mason Temple the night before he was killed. King insisted, in this address, that the collective pooling of resources in the black community was a viable means to power:

> the Negro collectively is richer than most nations of the world. We have an annual income of more than thirty billion dollars a year, which is more than all of the exports of the United States, and more than the national budget of Canada. Did you know that? That's power right there, if we know how to pool it.[16]

King also went on to state,

> "we've got to strengthen black institutions," and urged the audience to take their business to black institutions, "I call upon you to take your money out of the bank downtown and deposit your money in Tri-State Bank—we want a "bank-in" movement in Memphis. Put your money there. You have six or seven black insurance companies in Memphis. Take out your insurance there."[17]

Although King's philosophy often carried a populist motif, the themes of black self-reliance and black self-identity became more pronounced within the last year of his life.

In keeping with his philosophy of the movement as a whole, King saw that the demands of integration fell within the scope of "unenforceable demands" which "law books cannot regulate."[18] The laws governing integration, ultimately, did not have the capacity to set anyone free. King's philosophy of the movement was two-fold. He sought to exact a revolution of the mind and of the system simultaneously. He can be easily categorized as a pacifist, Christian existentialist or Hegelian personalist.[19] The demand for integration involved personal choice and "inner attitudes" and was essentially categorized as an ethical demand, according to King.[20] Martin Luther King, Jr. also saw history as a dialectical struggle between good and evil. He admittedly rejected the "superficial optimism" of protestant liberalism regarding human nature, for Hegel's cunning of reason. According to King, "reason was darkened by sin."[21]

For King, the most moral and logical *end* to history was the creation of the "beloved community."[22] King made the construction of a Beloved Community the primary goal of the SCLC. According to Ira G. Zepp, this was the "organizing principal of his life" and the philosophy of the movement.[23] As an integrated community of love, loyalty, brotherhood, and mutual respect, the "Beloved Community" was King's dream or an earthly extension of the "promised land." African Americans would never be free to inhabit this "beloved community" without gaining self-affirmation, because, "As long as the mind is enslaved, the body can never be free."[24] In order for black people to exist within this "Beloved Community," with *authenticity* and *commitment*, they would first have to undergo a process of psychological liberation." Black Power in the positive sense is a psychological call to manhood. This is desperately needed in the black community, because for all too many years black people have been ashamed of themselves."[25] King came to understand, in his last days, the call for Black Power as a bid for psychological freedom. He eventually came to the conclusion that any movement toward black equality must first acknowledge the need for black self-identity. King's most radical speech, couched in black consciousness, was given during the last convention he attended as President of SCLC in August 1967:

> The tendency to ignore the Negro's contribution to American life and to strip him of his personhood is as old as the earliest history books and as contemporary as the morning's newspaper. To upset this cultural homicide, the Negro must rise up with an affirmation of his own Olympian manhood. Any movement for the Negro's freedom that overlooks this necessity is only waiting to be buried.[26]

King did not sound quite like himself in this speech. He also went on to assert in this message that for black people in America freedom from self-abnegation was an integral part of the struggle for black equality:

> Psychological freedom, a firm sense of self-esteem, is the most powerful weapon against the long night of physical slavery. No Lincolnian emancipation proclamation or Johnsonian civil rights bill can totally bring this kind of freedom. The Negro will only be free when he reaches down in the inner depths of his own being and signs with the pen and ink of assertive manhood his own emancipation proclamation. . . . "Yes, we must stand up and say I'm black and I'm beautiful," and this self-affirmation is the black man's need, made compelling by the white man's crime against him.[27]

King's faith in the federal government faltered during his last days as witnessed much needed funds for social programs diverted to the war in Vietnam. This sparked his criticism of Lyndon Johnson's administration.

Martin Luther King, Jr. agreed with the basic precepts of Black Power, and moved closer to the radicals in the movement after 1966, with his denunciation of the war in Vietnam along with his conclusions on "black power." King saw the movement toward Black Power shift toward a Black Revolution, amid the backdrop of urban riots. He saw this as a likely outcome of the movement, "I am not sad that black Americans are rebelling; this was not only inevitable but eminently desirable."[28] In a speech given at the Riverside Church in New York City in April of 1967, King publicly "recommended" the alternative of "conscientious objection." He later described, in a posthumous essay, the Johnson administration as one "devoid of statesmanship" on Vietnam policy.[29]

The other moderates within the vanguard were not in complete agreement with King. King's philosophical interpretation of the movement, coupled with the strategy of nonviolent direct action, was most contrary to Roy Wilkin's pragmatic legal-gradualist approach to power for black Americans. While King saw that the law could not make black people completely free, Roy Wilkins believed that the law was an instrument that would gain black people the most freedom.

Many of the moderates within the coalition, along with the national press, looked upon the shift toward Black Power as an unfortunate time of crisis and confusion. Roy Wilkins described the situation:

> All about us are alarums and confusions as well as great and challenging developments. Differences of opinion are sharper. For the first time since several organizations began to function where only two had functioned before, there emerges what seems to be a difference in goals.[30]

The national press recognized a "crisis" as well, and the impending end of coalition. John K. Jessup, writing for one prominent magazine, insisted that "the Negro revolution has changed its character," and had become suddenly more "urgent."[31] Another periodical suggested that the call for "black power" was simply a part of the "racist philosophy" of separatism.[32] It was *Life* magazine that insisted Black Power *must* be defined, and that there was a "New Negro Mood" apparent, a mood "more militant and more race-conscious."[33] Jerry Cohen and William S. Murphy, members of the *Los Angeles Times* staff, and winners of the Pulitzer Prize for their coverage of the Watts Riots, were convinced that black extremists were preparing for "guerrilla warfare."[34] Russell Sackett was certain that the potential was great for a guerilla war, "In secret recesses of any ghetto in the U.S. there are dozens and hundreds of black men working resolutely toward an Armageddon in which Whitey is to be either destroyed or forced to his knees."[35] Martin Luther King Jr. expressed his concerns early on that, "the movement is very, very, close to a permanent split over the issue of black power."[36]

Bayard Rustin, a special advisor to King, and a representative of the A. Philip Randolph Institute, was concerned:

> within the Negro community itself, "black power" has touched off a major debate—the most bitter the community has experienced since the days of Booker T. Washington and W.E.B. Du Bois, and one which threatens to ravage the entire civil rights movement. Indeed, a serious split has already developed between advocates of black power like Floyd McKissick of CORE and Stokely Carmichael of SNCC, on the one hand, and Dr. Martin Luther King of SCLC, Roy Wilkins of the NAACP, and Whitney Young of the Urban League, on the Other.[37]

The Black Power debate delivered a tremendous blow to the continuation of the consensus for coalition. The collapse of coalition disabled the movement's broad transition from protest to *realpolitik*.

With the popularization of the phrase at Greenwood, Mississippi by Stokley Carmichael, there emerged an irrevocable split in the personality of the coalition, so described by one leading periodical:

> This brash new philosophy—chauvinistic, intolerant of compromise—has been wedging Negro leaders into two separate and increasingly hostile camps. On the right is the Movement's Establishment, the old, large and rich organizations like the National Association for the Advancement of Colored People and the Urban League that have manned and bankrolled the struggle for years past. Their leaders, Roy Wilkins of the NAACP and Whitney Young, Jr., of the Urban League, are skilled politicians of the possible: they want to push the cause as far as they can as fast as they can. But long experience has convinced them that progress is made with measured tread. On the left, rallied under the banners of black power, stand McKissick's CORE and Carmichael's SNCC. . . . To them, gradualism is an act of treason, and the old-line leaders—for the most part—are "Uncle Toms" tainted by long contact with the sinister "white-power structure."[38]

Most did not stretch their interpretation of the redemptive qualities of "black power" as far as King. Bayard Rustin, once King's closest aide, aligned himself with the quest for integration through coalition superceding racial, political and ideological conflicts. The ideal coalition for Rustin was a "liberal-labor-civil rights" alliance within the confines of the Democratic party. Rustin contended that the "propagation" of black power was "positively harmful" to the movement, while he championed the tool of political alliance at all costs. He claimed, "it was through alliances with other groups (in political machines or as part of the trade union movement) that the Irish and the Jews and the Italians acquired the power to win their rightful place in American society."[39] James Farmer, in his recollections of the movement, considered that, although pride in one's race was positive, the idea of "exclusive love" or power becomes sinister in a pluralistic society that should welcome and celebrate all cultures equally.[40] Farmer, amid CORE's new emphasis on the quest for "black power," resigned his post as National Director of CORE by fall 1966.

A. Philip Randolph, founder of the Brotherhood of Sleeping Car Porters, and father of the Civil Rights Movement, like Rustin, was an advocate of direct mass action through a coalition of reform minded groups. It became, not only a time of confusion, but a time of disorganized thinking about black.

The coalition was unable to reconcile itself, and split along the lines of integration and separation. The integrationists were on the defensive. The defenders of integration found themselves explaining *integration* in order to stave off a serious white backlash, as well as convince or calm black radicals by taking out a full page ad in the *New York Times* on October 14, 1966:

> We are committed to the attainment of racial justice by the democratic process. We are committed to integration, by which we mean an end to every barrier which segregation and other forms of discrimination have raised against the enjoyment by Negro Americans of their human and constitutional rights. We believe that a sense of personal worth and a pride in race are vital to integration in a pluralistic society, but we believe that these are best nurtured by success in achieving equality. We reject the way of separatism, either moral or spatial. We not only welcome, we urge, the full cooperation of white Americans.[41]

In a critique of integration, one black radical insisted that it was simply an "insidious subterfuge for the maintenance of white supremacy."[42] Julius Lester, a former SNCC field secretary, declared that integration was "only another variation on the theme of white supremacy," and that it has to mean a "denial of self."[43] Because their organizations were the largest, oldest, and most monetarily solvent, within the vanguard, Roy Wilkins's and Whitney Young's views on Black Power are most important here.

The National Association for the Advancement of Colored People, along with the National Urban League, existed as veritable juggernauts in the challenge for national civil rights reform. Their combined might had the potential to make or disrupt the consensus for coalition. The League, formed in 1911 to accommodate the growing influx of African Americans to the cities of the North, gained great prestige as primarily a social service and public policy agency. A volunteer and professional staff sustained it. Unlike the League, the NAACP was largely a membership organization. Responding to the rapid rise of Jim Crow, and to combat lynch law, the NAACP was formed in 1909 as a protest movement by black intellectuals and white liberals. By 1966, it was the oldest, largest, and most prestigious organization of all with a membership of nearly a half a million and a gross annual income of $1, 408, 385.[44] The Urban League experienced astronomical growth during the tenure of Whitney Young from 1961 to 1971. The League nearly doubled in size, increasing the number of affiliates from 63 to 98, with an annual income that increased from $310,000 to more than 10 million dollars.[45] The NAACP, under the direction of Roy Wilkins, and the Urban League, under the guidance of Whitney Young, had the capacity to invigorate or destroy the coalition for civil rights reform.

Roy Wilkins interpreted the movement in pragmatic legalisms, while Whitney Young counseled the practicality of persuasion. Both championed the strategy of legal maneuver and legislative measure to achieve integration. Roy Wilkins, the grandson of slaves was born in St. Louis, Missouri in 1901. Educated at the University of Minnesota, he initially trained as a journalist, forging his professional career with the NAACP from 1931 to 1977.[46] Whitney Young, born in Lincoln Ridge, Kentucky in 1921, shaped his career in the field of social work. Young, who served in World War II with the 369th regiment, graduated with a degree in pre-medicine from Kentucky State College in 1941, and later earned a graduate degree in Social Work from the University of Minnesota in 1947. He became involved with the League, as director of industrial relations with the St. Paul, Minnesota chapter, that same year.

"The legal battles would have been won in the courts without the marching," reflected Roy Wilkins on the strategy of nonviolent direct action utilized by King in Montgomery.[47] The NAACP did not officially endorse the methods of nonviolent direct action until 1960. But recognizing that the marching did provide a kind of "soul power" for the people involved, Wilkins reluctantly supported direct action for the common goal of the movement.

Integration through legislation had become the dominant policy of the NAACP by 1966. It was the policy readily championed by Wilkins:

> The N.A.A.C.P. was interested exclusively in securing first-class citizenship for Negro Americans as speedily as possible. We realized that the attainment of this object required the astute and unselfish use of a variety of methods, and we would continue to use all of them. But we believed that citizenship had to be firmly secured in law, or it would become a whimsical thing, dependent on local or regional happenstance . . . the meat and potatoes had to be citizenship protected by law.[48]

Roy Wilkins considered legal moves to be the foundation on which the movement hinged, hence his reluctance to endorse direct action: "Affirmative action by judicial, legislative and executive means is indispensable. This is still a nation of law. If we colored people hold the white people of the South to the law and the Constitution, we cannot sneer among ourselves at the law and the legal processes."[49] Wilkins described the Civil Rights Act of 1964 as the "Magna Carta for the race," and as a "splendid monument for the cause of human rights."[50] According to Wilkins, the most feasible means to black equality was operating within the confines of the law and the American system. The black reality was an American reality:

> The leadership that recognizes the Negro as an American who has been on this continent for 345 years and must, therefore, attain his heritage as an American is the leadership in tune with reality. As uncertain and despairing as that reality may seem at times under the ministrations of the majority and the interpretations of the black prophets of gloom and desperation, it is nevertheless the only

feasible way now discernible.[51]

"All pragmatists counsel hard thinking and unremitting use of the available pressures," stated Wilkins early in 1966.[52] Roy Wilkins remained the pragmatist regarding the call for "black power."

"It has to mean separatism," this is how Roy Wilkins described "black power."[53] The ideology of separatism, as understood by Wilkins, was a backward and negative response, in the struggle for black equality, which had nothing to offer black Americans in the long run. He characterized separatism in such terms, "black separatism is black group suicide."[54] Roy Wilkins categorized the proponents of Black Power as "black racists," "black know-nothings," "disruptors," and "don't give-a-damn hate white-people preachers," within his columns which appeared in the *Amsterdam News* and the *Daily News* between the years 1966 and 1968. These advocates, with their "tough talk," and "boasting of power they do not have," were hurting the movement overall as well as "doing damage to our children," according to Wilkins.[55] Roy Wilkins believed the call for "black power," which he equated with black separatism, to be contrary to the goals of the NAACP, and the movement as a whole. In 1966, during his keynote address, he told the delegates to the 57th annual convention of the Association that, "We of the NAACP will have none of this."[56]

Roy Wilkins offered a continuous, and largely consistent, scathing critique of "black power," and the radical dissent that fueled it. He publicly distanced the goals of the NAACP away from SNCC, away from "black power," and subsequently away from the coalition:

> No matter how endlessly they try to explain it, the term 'black power' means anti-white power. In a racially pluralistic society, the concept, the formation and the exercise of an ethnically-tagged power means opposition to other ethnic powers, just as the term 'white supremacy' means subjection of all non-white people. In the black-white relationship, it has to mean that every other ethnic power is the rival and the antagonist of 'black power.' It has to mean 'going-it-alone.' It has to mean separatism. Now, separatism, whether on the rarified level of a secessionist Freedom City in Watts, offers a disadvantaged minority little except the chance to shrivel up and die.[57]

With this statement, Wilkins denied the fact that America, as a pluralistic society, is *in fact* a society comprised of contentious racial, ethnic, and religious power blocs. The story of the American experience, especially the quest for political power, has involved competition amongst these groups—along with the modern introduction of some new "special interests." Roy Wilkins immediately denied a certain segment, the nationalist strain of black protest thought, an "ethnic conception of reality." For Wilkins, Black Power became black separatism. The goals of the NAACP were different:

> We seek, therefore, as we have sought these many years, for the inclusion of Negro Americans in the nation's life, not their exclusion. This is our land, as

much so as it is any American's—every square foot of every city and town and village. The task of winning our share is not the easy one of disengagement and flight.[58]

The philosophy of separatism had previously failed in black America, according to Wilkins. He was seconded in his opinion by Whitney Young. Young believed that black people were already separate, and this was the great cause of their problems.

Whitney M. Young, Jr. was able to "persuade" much of the white power structure to invest in black progress through the means of philanthropic endeavor. Major funding for the League came through foundation grants and through the support of federal dollars. The Rockefeller Foundation was one of the League's major benefactors. Young came to lead the organization, abandoning his post as dean of the Atlanta University School of Social Work, in 1961. Although the National Urban League can be considered perhaps the most conservative organization within the group, under the tutelage of Young, from 1961-1971, the League became more aggressive in the pursuit of social justice in matters concerning education, the work-place, and overall civil rights issues.

Whitney Young was a believer in the American creed of equality and justice for all. He repeatedly defined the movement as a struggle to obtain the full benefits of American citizenship, "This is a revolution peculiarly characterized by a heroic drive and a courageous fight to gain the rights and respect that should be synonymous with the word American."[59] As with Wilkins, for Young the object of Black Power was for African Americans to become equal partners within the mainstream of American life, "I believe in the need for an integrated society, not because associating with whites is, of itself, a good thing, but because it is only through participation in the mainstream that full equality can be won."[60] The Urban League, through the instigations of Young, implemented the strategy of improving the social conditions of African Americans through on the job training programs, educational assistance programs, and by providing employment placement opportunities.

Young, having been criticized for his group's lack of visible participation in mass protest action, defined direct action as "putting a man in a job."[61] During the tenure of Young, through such endeavors as the National Skills Bank, the On-the-Job training program, and the Broadcast Skills Bank, the League provided new skills and new job opportunities for blacks in industry. The On-the-Job Training program, which placed unskilled workers into training programs in private industry, was funded by a contract from the Department of Labor that managed to make significant gains in black employment totaling 50,000 in seven years; the annual reports of the League indicated more than 40,000 job placements per year.[62] Young implemented vocational education projects, individualized tutoring for black youths, and thus considered the meaning of "black power" in such a way, "Any phrase which means all things to all people becomes meaningless. Power is neither black nor white—it is the green of the dollar bill, the maroon of a text book and the gray of a pay envelope."[63] Young's philosophy of the movement, with an emphasis in improving education, and achieving employment equity, was perhaps closest to that of A. Philip Randolph.

Confronted by black radical dissent, both Roy Wilkins and Whitney Young were forced to defend the meaning of integration. The term integration became to some associated with the relinquishment of one's racial identity or the attempt to emulate white Americans. "Black Power," to the integrationists, became defined as separatist. The various forms of separatism, cultural, economic, and territorial, became, to the defenders of integration, nothing more than symbolic of a black failure to compete within mainstream American life. Things thus became disorganized, at the expense of coalition. The debate concerning Black Power became inextricably linked with the search for black identity. While Wilkins described integration as "inclusion" into the mainstream of American life, Young championed the need for an open society noting that, "Integration does not imply rejection of black values or a desire to imitate white society. If anything, belief in an open society affirms a belief that black people can compete on an equal basis with whites."[64]

Although Young succinctly criticized territorial separatism, he did describe the idea of a separate economy for blacks as a "marginal substitute" for the wealth and power to be found in the American system. He chose to eventually reinterpret the need for Black Power. The League's New Thrust project, begun in 1968, focused upon "building the strength and power of the black ghetto, developing creative confrontations to produce basic system changes, and pressing for full-scale integration."[65] As Martin Luther King, Jr. selected to embrace the basic agenda of Black Power, and Whitney Young made a late attempt to reinterpret the concept, Roy Wilkins steadfastly held it in contempt.

Although they argued to the contrary, many of the integrationist precepts for black empowerment suggested black assimilation into the "American mainstream." The ability to maintain black cultural attributes increasingly entered into the broad debate for black equality and Black Power. On the other hand the great misconception, on the part of the integrationists, was to equate "black power" as simply black separatism—as if there were no other credible meaning for it. Though Malcolm X was a territorial separatist, emerging radical leaders from the coalition, such as Stokely Carmichael and Floyd McKissick, were political pluralists.

Notes

1 Peter Ling, "Martin Luther King's Half-Forgotten Dream," *History Today*, April, 1998, 17. The most recent historical scholarship, regarding the role of King in the movement, as Ling suggests in this article, indicts the "King-centric popular literature" for a false perception of the movement: King was the movement's most cherished spokesman, but there is credence to the fact that it was the activism of SNCC and CORE which shaped the movement as a whole.

2 The Southern Christian Leadership Conference, officially formed in the early Winter of 1957, was made up of a loose confederation of local black ministers many of whom had ties with the NAACP.

3 Stephen B. Oates, *Let the Trumpet Sound: A Life of Martin Luther King, Jr.* (New York: Harper & Row, 1982), 68-70.

4 The product of a middle class Christian fundamentalist upbringing, King, in his formative years, attended David T. Howard Elementary School, Atlanta University Laboratory School, and Booker T. Washington High School between the years of 1935 to 1944. During these years he skipped several grades, which enabled him to enter Moorehouse College at the age of fourteen.

5 Nixon, a Sleeping Car Porter, was a leading member of the Alabama chapter of the NAACP.

6 Adam Fairclough, *To Redeem the Soul of America: The Southern Christian Leadership Conference and Martin Luther King, Jr.* (Athens & London: University of Georgia Press, 1987), 5-6.

7 James Meredith, who integrated the University of Mississippi in 1962 under the protection of federal marshals, made an attempt to march from Memphis, Tennessee to Jackson, Mississippi, "without fear" but was felled by 27 pellets of buck-shot on June 6, 1966. The coalition came to continue the march under the direction of King.

8 According to the recollections of SNCC activist Cleveland Sellers, "Wilkins and Young were furious" at the idea of an "all black" emphasis on the march.

9 "Dr. King Receives $100,000 Donation," *New York Times*, 6 July 1966, 15. King's initial public response was that the term *black power* "connotes black supremacy and an anti-white feeling" as well as implications of "black nationalism."

10 Martin Luther King, Jr., "Where Do We Go From Here: Chaos or Community?" in *A Testament of Hope: The Essential Writings And Speeches of Martin Luther King, Jr.*, ed. James Washington, (1986; New York: Harper Collins, 1991), 574.

11 Gene Roberts, "King Stresses Pride in His Race," *New York Times*, 19 Aug. 1967: 12. Placards posted at the last convention King attended for his organization stated, "Black is Beautiful and Its So Beautiful to Be Black." The tone of his convention speech reflected similar sentiments.

12 Martin Luther King, Jr., "Where Do We Go From Here?," in *A Testament of Hope: The Essential Writings of Martin Luther King, Jr.*, ed. James Washington, (1986; New York: Harper Collins, 1991), 246.

13 Martin Luther King, Jr., "Black Power Defined," in *A Testament of Hope: The Essential Writings of Martin Luther King, Jr.*, ed. James Washington, (1986; New York, Harper Collins, 1991), 312.

14 Martin Luther King, Jr., "Black Power Defined," in *Testament of Hope*, 303.

15 Martin Luther King, Jr., "Where Do We Go From Here: Chaos or Community?" in *Testament of Hope*, 577-578.

16 Martin Luther King, Jr., "I See the Promised Land," in *Testament of Hope*, 283.

17 Ibid.

18 Martin Luther King, Jr. "The Ethical Demands For Integration," in *Testament of Hope*, 123.

19 King's God was more personal, rather than the God of Hegel's abstract Idea.

20 King relates, in his essay "Pilgrimage to Nonviolence," that the existentialist assertions on anxiety, conflict, the finite freedom of man, and the threat of meaninglessness, had a profound influence on his philosophical development; this is evidenced throughout his general protest ethic.

21 Martin Luther King, Jr. "Pilgrimage to Nonviolence," in *Testament of Hope*, 36.

22 We find the analogy of the Beloved Community, a direct notion of the American philosopher Josiah Royce (1855-19160, who in his writings emphasized a doctrine of loyalty through a "beloved community," in many of Kings philosophical musings. Like Royce before him, King came to understand Christianity as *the* religion of love, loyalty, and brotherhood which had the potential to bind people together in a "beloved community."

23 Ira G. Zepp, Jr., *The Social Vision of Martin Luther King, Jr.* (New York: Carlson Publishing, 1989), 207.

24 Martin Luther King, Jr., "Where Do We Go From Here?" in *Testament of Hope*, 246.

25 Martin Luther King, Jr., in response to Rabbi Everett Gendler on March 25, 1968, "Conversation with Martin Luther King," in *Testament of Hope*, 663.

26 Martin Luther King, Jr., "Where Do We Go From Here?" in *Testament of Hope*, 246.

27 Ibid.

28 Martin Luther King, Jr. "Testament of Hope," in *Testament of Hope*, 313.

29 Ibid.

30 Roy Wilkins, "Keynote Address of Roy Wilkins, Executive Director National Association for the Advancement of Colored People before its Fifty-Seventh Annual Convention," July 5, 1966, *The NAACP Papers-Part IV, 1966-1973* (Washington, D.C., The Library of Congress) Box A3, Folder 6.

31 John K. Jessup, "An Urgent New Reach to be Equal," *Life*, June 3, 1966, 88.

32 "The New Racism," *Time*, July 1, 1966, 11.

33 "The New Negro Mood," *Life*, June 10, 1966, 4.

34 Jerry Cohen, and William S. Murphy, "Burn, Baby, Burn!" *Life*, July 15, 1966, 46.

35 Russell Sackett, "Plotting A War On Whitey: If Negro Leadership Fails, Extremists Are Set and Eager for Violence," *Life*, June 10, 1966, 100.

36 "At the Breaking Point," *Time*, July 15, 1966, 15.

37 Bayard Rustin, "Black Power and Coalition Politics," *Down the Line: The Selected Writings of Bayard Rustin* (Chicago: Quadrangle Books, 1971), 154.

38 "Black Power: Road to Disaster?" *Newsweek*, August 22, 1966, 32.

39 Rustin, "Black Power and Coalition Politics," in *Down the Line*, 156.

40 James Farmer, *Lay Bare the Heart: An Autobiography of the Civil Rights Movement* (Fort Worth: Texas Christian University Press, 1998), 306.

41 "Crisis And Commitment," *Crisis*, (November 1966): 475. This document, reprinted in the NAACP's monthly magazine, had several signers who defended the integrationist approach to power including Bayard Rustin, Dorothy Height, Roy Wilkins, and Whitney Young.

42 "Stokely Carmichael, "Black Power," in *Black Protest: 350 Years of History, Documents, And Analyses,* ed. Joanne Grant, (1968; New York, 1996.), 435.

43 Julius Lester, "The Necessity For Separation," *Ebony*, August, 1970, 168.

44 "NAACP Annual Meeting," *Crisis*, (January 1966): 10-12.

45 Nancy J. Weiss, "Whitney M. Young, Jr.: Committing the Power Structure to the Cause of Civil Rights," in *Black Leaders of the Twentieth Century*, ed. John Hope Franklin and August Meier, (Urbana and Chicago: University of Illinois Press, 1982) 336.

46 Wilkins served as editor of the *Crisis*, assistant secretary, executive secretary, and executive director during his 46 years of tenure with the NAACP.

47 Roy Wilkins, with Tom Mathews, *Standing Fast: The Autobiography of Roy Wilkins* (1982; New York: Da Capo Press, 1994), 237.

48 Wilkins, in *Standing Fast*, 270.

49 Roy Wilkins, "For Shock Troops and Solid Legal Moves," in *Black Protest Thought in the Twentieth Century,* ed. August Meier, (Indianapolis and New York: The Bobbs Merrill Company, Inc., 1971), 321.

50 Wilkins, in *Standing Fast*, 302.

51 Roy Wilkins, "What Now?-One Negro Leaders Answer," August 16, 1964, *The Papers of Roy Wilkins* (Washington, D.C.: the Library of Congress) Box 37, Folder A6.

52 Roy Wilkins, "The Disrupters," April 24, 1966, *The Papers of Roy Wilkins* (Washington, D.C.: The Library of Congress) Box 39, Folder 5.

53 Roy Wilkins, "Keynote Address of Roy Wilkins, Executive Director National Association for the Advancement of Colored People before its Fifty-Seventy Annual Convention," July 5, 1966, *The NAACP Papers-Part IV: 1966-1973* (Washington, D.C.: The Library of Congress) Box A3, Folder 6.

54 Roy Wilkins, "SNCC's New Road," June 4, 1966, *The Papers of Roy Wilkins* (Washington, D.C.: The Library of Congress) Box 39, Folder 5.

55 Roy Wilkins, "Damage To Our Children," July 23, 1966, *The Papers of Roy Wilkins* (Washington, D.C.: The Library of Congress) Box 39, Folder 4.

56 Roy Wilkins, in "Keynote Address," *Roy Wilkins Papers*, at the Library of Congress, Box A3, Folder 6.

57 Ibid.

58 Ibid.

59 Whitney M. Young, Jr., "For Protest Plus Corrective Measures," in *Black Protest Thought in the Twentieth Century,* ed. August Meier, (Indianapolis and New York: The Bobbs Merrill Company, Inc., 1971), 324.

60 Whitney M. Young, Jr., "We Are Separated That's the Cause of All Our Woes," *Ebony*, August, 1970, 91.

61 "Urban League Chief Deplores the Fight Over Black Power," *New York Times,* August 5, 1966, 10.

62 Nancy J. Weiss, "Whitney M. Young, Jr.: Committing the Power Structure to the Cause of Civil Rights," in John Hope Franklin, in *Black Leaders of the Twentieth Century*, ed. August Meier, (Urbana and Chicago: University of Illinois Press, 1982), 335.

63 M.S. Handler, "Whitney Young Urges Attempt be Made to Reach Ghetto Unreachables," *New York Times,* August 1, 1966, 14.

64 Whitney M. Young, Jr., "We Are Separated That's the Cause of All Our Woes," *Ebony*, August 1970, 96.

65 National Urban League, "Implementing A New Thrust for the Urban League Movement," *Papers of the National Urban League: Part III (1966-1979)*, June. 7, 1968, (Washington, D.C.: The Library of Congress) Box 35, Folder 11.

Chapter 3

The Devil is White

White devil wid pitch forks
Threw black devils on,
Slim thought he'd better
Be gittin along.
Sterling Brown, "Slim in Hell"

"This Caucasian devil slave-master does not want or trust us to leave him—yet when we stay here among him, he continues to keep us at the very lowest level of his society," once stated Malcolm X.[1] For quite some time, Malcolm X believed that the devil was white. He was the main catalyst in stoking the fires of black radical dissent, a transitional figure, as the movement for civil rights reform evolved into the Black Revolution. If Martin Luther King, Jr. was at the center of the movement for national civil rights reform, Malcolm X was situated at the center of the Black Revolution. The Black Studies scholar William L. Van De burg has proclaimed that Malcolm X was *the* paradigm for Black Power:

> Following his death, Malcolm's influence expanded in dramatic, almost loga-
> rithmic, fashion. He came to be far more than a martyr for the militant, separa-
> tist faith. He became a Black Power paradigm—the archetype, reference point,
> and spiritual advisor in absentia for a generation of Afro-American activists.
> Although diverse in manner and mode of expression, it was the collective thrust
> of these activists toward racial pride, strength, and self-definition that came to
> be called the Black Power movement.[2]

According to Amiri Baraka, the dissent of black radicals away from coalition, into a movement for black self-identity and self-determinism, was propelled by the "catalyzed militancy" of Malcolm X.[3] Malcolm X had a profound impact in shaping the radical-militant mindset in the 1960s.

Although the "post-Mecca" Malcolm abandoned territorial separatism, he did not relinquish Black Nationalism. Within the *Black Power paradigm*, under the umbrella of "separatists," we can include territorial nationalists, Pan-Africanists, Pan-Caribbeanists and cultural nationalists. Under the column of experimentalists, we can include revolutionary nationalists and black socialists. Malcolm X, before and after his trip to Mecca, remained a black nationalist. He continued to be an outspoken champion of black self-determinism and self-identity.

The main purpose of this chapter is to explain the separatist impulse, as chiefly articulated by Malcolm X. Dormant or active, the separatist impulse has survived in black culture, custom, and in black protest thought. Most black people in America today, whether they live in a predominantly white neighborhood, or in the black ghetto, wear a cloak of separateness everyday—this "cloak" is their dark skin. The very fact that black people have always *been different* has simply reinforced this feeling. Phillis Wheatley described her very different experience, as a slave in eighteenth century America, with feelings of "tyrannic sway."[4] Claude McKay, a poet of the Harlem Renaissance, discussed the black existence in America as "The Negro's Tragedy," separate, and hidden within the "thickness of the shroud of night."[5] The post-modern poet Nikki Giovanni has related the state of being and feeling as if a separate *thing*, in a recent poem, as a riot that "is all day everyday."[6] The state of *being* and feeling separate, as if a separate thing, has distinctly shaped black nationalist ideology. As James Turner has said, "The black nationalist recognizes himself as belonging to an out-group, an alien in relation to the white society which controls the total universe in which he moves."[7] Because, as James Baldwin has told us, "the universe has evolved no terms" for a black existence in America, the themes of self-identity and self-determinism, through territorial, political, or cultural expression, have become the focal point of one particular segment of black protest thought: black separatism.

Due to historical circumstance, black Americans have been virtually locked into a state of perpetual separatism (either cultural or social) as a result of the social reality of race and the practice of racism in America. This predicament has engendered, "a counter-movement away from subordination to independence, from alienation through refutation, to eventual self-affirmation."[8] A great sense of alienation has evolved within the black community, through personal experiences, combined with an historic legacy as the descendants of slaves, and fostered through an enforced separation from whites predicated heavily upon the degradation of black. Regeneration through refutation, based in self-identification, has been the separatist response from Martin Delaney to Elijah Muhammad. The purpose of this chapter is to explore the separatist impulse in the 1960s, as chiefly articulated by Malcolm X, and Malcolm's influence in shaping the radical militant mindset. Before we can understand the separatism of Malcolm X, and others in the 1960s, a brief examination of Elijah Muhammad and the Nation of Islam is necessary.

The contemporary version of the Nation of Islam can be described as a social, religious, and business organization with political aspirations as articulated by Louis Farrakhan. Historically, it has been an organization rift with schisms from its inception.[9] Unfortunately, the "rift" between Elijah Muhammad and Malcolm X resulted in the brutal murder of the "post-Mecca" Malcolm who denounced territorial separatism. Malcolm X can be looked upon as one of the most maligned and misunderstood characters within the context of recent American history, but to understand Malcolm is to understand the Black Power paradigm. And to understand Malcolm's "separatism," we must first take a look at the Nation of Islam.

Elijah Muhammad operated his organization as a veritable nation in waiting from 1933, until his death in 1975. Before Malcolm joined the NOI, Elijah

Poole, the former Detroit auto worker born in Sandersville, Georgia in 1898, had changed his last name to Muhammad and appointed himself the sole interpreter of Allah's word by founder Wallace D. Fard. With the disappearance of Fard in 1933, Elijah Muhammad subsequently deified Fard as the incarnation of God on earth and presented himself as the "messenger" or principle apostle of Fard [God]. The Islamic oriented nationalism of W.D. Fard, as originally derived from the teachings of Timothy Drew [Noble Drew Ali], and combined with the later influence of Garveyism, became the foundations of the theocratic patriarchy cultivated and envisioned by Elijah Muhammad. Muhammad's "nation in waiting" comprised several business enterprises, maintained an internal taxation system called the "duty," retained a uniformed security force known as the Fruits of Islam, and had its own independent Islamic flag.

It was Fard, who some have suggested was a former Garveyite, who emphasized the ideology of the "white devil." With the death of the Noble Drew Ali in 1929, W.D. Fard deviated from the central precepts of Drew which emphasized a nationalist identity more in line with an Asiatic or Moorish and Islamic identity.[10] The foundation of Elijah Muhammad's organization, created by Fard, were derived from the split within Timothy Drew's organization known as the Moorish Science Temple first established in Newark, New Jersey of 1913. Fard's Muslim Cult of Islam became the Nation of Islam under Elijah Muhammad after 1933.

The entrepreneurship of Elijah Muhammad was similar to the endeavors of Marcus Garvey in the 1920s. Through his Universal Negro Improvement Association (UNIA), Garvey sustained such business endeavors as the Black Star Shipping Line and the Negro Factories Corporation, which employed hundreds of blacks in the New York area in such businesses as a steam laundry and a doll factory. The newspapers *The Negro World* in New York and the *Blackman* in Jamaica were also ambitious business endeavors of the UNIA. With chapters in over forty countries, with 700 in America alone and nearly 300 abroad, the UNIA had a significant influence within the black community in America during the 1920s.[11] The Nation of Islam, under Elijah Muhammad, became the most legitimate successor to Marcus Garvey and the Universal Negro Improvement Association. By the mid 1950s Muhammad had created for his "nation in waiting" an economic infrastructure which included schools [the University of Islam], grocery stores, the Moslem Farm Market, supported by a 140 acre farm in White Cloud, Michigan, an auto repair shop, a laundry, and restaurants, along with dress stores and some haberdashery establishments.[12] The Nation of Islam also published newspapers called *Muhammad Speaks,* and *The Final Call.*

The basic tenets of Elijah Muhammad's separatism can be interpreted as a process or gradual preparation toward a separate, territorial, national identity for black Americans. Elijah Muhammad looked *toward* a separate national identity inside, or outside of, the boarders of the United States. As head of the NOI from 1934 to 1975, Elijah Muhammad insisted that the black race was to be venerated above the white. He also believed that separatism was an expression of black survival, self-love, dignity, and unity. A separate national identity was essentially the most positive expression of black independence according to Elijah Muhammad. The Black Muslim program consisted of a fusion of religious mysticism derived from Fard, coupled with some of the tenets of traditional Islam, territorial separatism, and economic nationalism. Members were encouraged to prepare themselves for the separation that was to come, as they were barred from serving in the U.S. military, voting in U.S. elections, or acquiring a social security number. Each member was obligated to pay their "duty" to support the Nation's infrastructure. In 1942, Muhammad was charged with sedition for protesting the war, and refusing to register with the draft, and subsequently served a four year prison term.

The Nation of Islam was guided by the ingrained precepts that (1) blacks were the original people on earth, and American blacks were descendants of the Asian black nation of Shabazz, (2) whites were their opposite, and should be considered devils with conniving ways, as they were created by the "evil" scientist Yakub as an artificial mutation of the original black man, and that (3) through self-knowledge and self-help, national black sovereignty was possible. Elijah Muhammad spread his influence throughout urban black America, and transformed a once obscure religious sect into a significant business enterprise and mass social organization. The estimated net worth of the Nation of Islam, at the death of Elijah Muhammad, was set at nearly 50 million dollars in assets by 1975.[13]

Malcolm X believed what the "messenger" Muhammad told him. He believed that the devil was white. Born in Omaha, Nebraska of 1925, to a mulatto mother and a father who was a Baptist minister and Garveyite, Malcolm Little was swayed by the teachings of Elijah Muhammad while serving six years of a prison term, for burglary. During his tenure as a Minister with the Nation of Islam [1952-1964], Malcolm X clung tenaciously to the doctrine of separatism. He was *the* quintessential prophet of black hate and one of the most mesmerizing articulators of black rage. His hatred of the "blue eyed devils" was made profoundly clear. In his autobiography, as told to Alex Haley, Malcolm X tells us he believed wholeheartedly in the idea of separatism, as represented by Elijah Muhammad, and that the teachings of the "messenger" Muhammad were represented by him. Malcolm tells us he believed in the doctrine of separatism, and he taught it fervently as he stated, "Anyone who has listened to me will have to agree that I believed in Elijah Muhammad and represented him one hundred percent."[14] As Muhammad taught his converts, Malcolm X preached that the only way for blacks to be "saved" was to separate from American society into a territory of their own. In his debates with James Farmer and Floyd McKissick, Malcolm X defended the separatist impulse.

According to Malcolm X, there was no hope in the American dream for black people. He had no confidence in the white man's willingness to allow blacks to integrate into white society, and because of this he stated, "we want to face the fact of the problems the way they are, and separate ourselves."[15] To him the American dream, for black people, was essentially an American nightmare. Most separatists, like Malcolm X, had very little or no faith in the redemptive qualities of the American system. While the integrationists believed in the potential of the essential values of American democracy, the separatists denied that the traditional values of the American system could ever pertain to them. There is a broad tapestry of nihilism woven into the fabric of the separatist impulse in black protest thought.

Within the Black Power paradigm, there are parallel and corresponding ideologies. It is a shifting paradigm. Some pluralists used a strategy of separatism to adapt to the American system, while separatists such as Elijah Muhammad used the tool of ethnic entrepreneurship as a model for the attainment of "black power." Malcolm X "shifts" with the paradigm. He described his life as a "chronology of change" in his autobiography. The chronology of change for Malcolm X involved a transition from street thug, to passionate black separatist, to a Sunni Islamic convert which included a renunciation of separatism. Malcolm X, with his return from Mecca in 1964, became vividly aware of the universality of Islam and the universal relevance of the black struggle in America, thereby shifting from black separatism to revolutionary Black Nationalism. Having abandoned his stance as a separatist, Malcolm X, at the time of his death in 1965, can be categorized as an experimentalist.

Malcolm clearly came to the conclusion that American society would have to be radically changed in order to become inclusive. His organizations, Muslim Mosque Incorporated and the Organization of African American Unity, created after his resignation from the NOI, were black nationalist in nature. All black nationalists were not territorial separatists, although the separatists and the experimentalists, and sometimes the pluralists, tended to operate from the same frame of reference which was in essence nationalist. Stokely Carmichael was essentially a pluralist, who flirted with experimentalism, and finally embraced Pan-Africanism. And Yusufu Sonebeyatta of the Republic of New Africa combined "experimental" black socialism, or African socialism, with separatism; his black state, encompassing counties across the South with large black populations in the states of Mississippi and Alabama among others, would be a separatist construct.[16]

The integrationists did not exist within a monolith of thought, nor did the separatists. Martin Luther King's tactics of non-violent direct action did not coincide with the legal gradualism of Roy Wilkins who admittedly believed, as stated in his autobiography, that the quest for black equality could have been won "without the marching." Elijah Muhammad's vision of a separatist patriarchal theocracy was certainly not synonymous with Sonebeyatta's socialist oriented vision of the black state. The pluralism of Floyd McKissick, as illustrated by his concept of "soul city,"[17] came closer to separatism, unlike the pluralism of Thomas W. Matthew of NEGRO (National Economic Growth and Reconstruction Organization) who emphasized ethnic entrepreneurship as the most constructive means to integration. And among separatists, we can legitimately include cultural nationalists, territorial nationalists, and economic nationalists.

As separatists, the cultural nationalists devalued the dominant Euro-American culture, and venerated a definitive Afrocentric culture as the true heritage of American blacks. Black culture, based in African tradition, was the most viable agent for liberation. Cultural nationalists such as Amiri Baraka and Ron Karenga, the originator of Kwanzaa, and member of US believed that a definitive cultural recognition would lead to economic endeavor and political change. Of course, revolutionary nationalists such as Huey P. Newton, who over emphasized the economic and political process to black liberation, considered cultural nationalism "pork chop nationalism."[18] Malcolm X embraced black culture, political organization, and ethnic entrepreneurship within his protest ethic. To understand Malcolm, is to understand the Black Power paradigm. But before his transition, Malcolm X was first and foremost the leading spokesperson for black separatism.

Many black separatists did not consider themselves racists, but simply pro-black operating for the best interests of all blacks. However Malcolm X further felt that the devil was white. Malcolm X understood separatism as something distinctly different from segregation. The writings of Elijah Muhammad would seem to suggest that the black nation state would include reciprocal trade with the white world as well as reciprocal tourism. He also suggested that the provisions of "reparation" owed to the black man would help to sustain this state as outlined in his 1965 text *Message to the Black Man in America*. Malcolm articulated the difference between separatism and segregation, as was taught to him by Elijah Muhammad, in his autobiography,

> To segregate means to control. Segregation is that which is forced upon inferiors by superiors. But *separation* is that which is done voluntarily, by two equals—for the good of both! The Honorable Elijah Muhammad teaches us that as long as our people here in America are dependent upon the white man, we will always be begging him for jobs, food, clothing, and housing. And he will always control our lives, regulate our lives, and have the power to segregate us. The Negro here in America has been treated like a child. A child stays within the mother until the time of birth! When the time of birth arrives, the child must be separated, or it will *destroy* its mother and itself.[19]

According to Malcolm X, only through separation and on their own terms would black people best obtain full equality. Black separatism, having little or nothing at all to do with black domination over white people, was articulated as a way in which black people would gain dominion over themselves. This was not possible in a society maintained by a white supremacist belief system predicated upon the degradation of black, according to the separatist mindset. Malcolm also clearly saw the movement for black equality, as a movement for human identity and human rights.

Black self identity was a major motif within the separatist impulse. In the ideal black state, African Americans would be able to live in equality with whites and have positive self images. Malcolm X was concerned with the lack of black identity and its coercive influence on black people, leading to the degradation of black in America. He warned that, "It is not integration that Negroes in

America want, it is human dignity. They want to be recognized as human beings." It was because the black man had been "robbed of his self," that an attempt was made, through integration, "to accept a white self," a premise totally unacceptable to Malcolm.[20] The theme of regeneration through self-affirmation, which was to be found in separation, was well pronounced in Malcolm's protest ethic. He preached that it was the black man who had been "mentally colonized:"

> his mind has been destroyed. And today, even though he goes to college, he comes out and still doesn't even know he is a black man; he is ashamed of what he is, because his culture has been destroyed, his identity has been destroyed; he has been made to hate his black skin, he has been made to hate the texture of his hair, he has been made to hate the features that God gave him.[21]

It was Malcolm who carried the torch of transition, as the movement for civil rights reform transformed into the push for black self identity and cultural revolution.

If Roy Wilkins adopted a gradual approach to integration, favoring the tactics of legal challenge and legislative maneuvering, then Elijah Muhammad adopted a gradual approach towards separation through the tactic of independent black organization. But unlike Elijah Muhammad, a political conservative who envisioned a peaceful petition for separation, the political radicalism and militant rhetoric of Malcolm X illustrated a quest for expeditious and thoroughgoing change through "any means necessary." Malcolm's political radicalism clashed with the political conservatism of the Messenger Muhammad. It challenged his authority, and threatened his yoke on the NOI which had become a mass organization and viable business conglomerate. The paternalistic patriarchal authority of Elijah Muhammad was vigorously challenged by the stature of Malcolm X. The young upstart that Muhammad had rescued from the gallows had, by the time of his death in 1965, created a dissension within the ranks.[22] Clearly, Elijah Muhammad was not a revolutionary nationalist who sought the violent political overthrow of the American government, nor did he seek a fundamental change to the American system. What Elijah Muhammad wanted was to first create the foundations of a black nation state through black self-reliance, then present a plan of reasonable partition or separation. Before we can explore more deeply the "evolution" of Malcolm X away from the NOI, we must examine the radical—militant mindset and the influence of Malcolm upon others within and peripheral to the vanguard.

Many African Americans, along with Malcolm X, began to become vocally cognizant of the fact that black Americans were simply *black people in America*. Malcolm X was perhaps one of the most influential articulators of this image. In a speech given after his departure from the NOI in 1964, he made this assertion poignantly clear:

> Being here in America doesn't make you American. Being born here in Amer-

ica doesn't make you an American. I'm one of the 22 million black people who
are the victims of democracy, nothing but disguised hypocrisy. So, I'm not
standing here speaking to you as an American. . . . I'm speaking as a victim of
this American system. And I see America through the eyes of the victim. I
don't see any American dream; I see an American nightmare.[23]

The militant-radical mindset of black activists was undeniably shaped by the
diatribes of Malcolm X and the writings of Frantz Fanon. Fanon divided the
colonial world into two compartments, the white world of the settler and the
black world of the native. According to Fanon there existed a deep contrast between these two worlds, "the zone where the natives live is not complementary
to the zone inhabited by the settlers, the settler's town is a well fed town, an
easygoing town; its belly is always full of good things. The native town is a
hungry town, starved of bread, of meat, of shoes, of coal, of light."[24]

Robert F. Williams, Stokely Carmichael, and Huey Newton continuously
referred to black people in America as "colonial subjects" in their musings on
black liberation. It was H. Rap Brown, Chairman of SNCC in 1967, who said
that black people were simply a part of the "colonized minorities" in America.[25]
Black radicals and militants considered that they lived in the "native" world of
which Fanon spoke. It became a serious goal to those in SNCC and CORE, sta-
tioned within the rural south, to foster a complete overthrow of segregation in
the south, both on the political and the economic scale. The theme of the "colonized" was adapted to the rhetoric of black militants and radicals, as they were
convinced that they simply were black and *in* America but not yet Americans.
They spoke of the plight of blacks as virtual refugees in America, trapped within
a "white city," reminiscent of the ponderings of the Harlem Renaissance poets
Langston Hughes and Claude McKay.

One of the brashest commentators on the theme of the colonized was Huey
P. Newton of the Black Panther Party:

> Penned up in the ghettos of America, surrounded by his factories and all the
> physical components of his economic system, we have been made into "the
> wretched of the earth," relegated to the position of spectators while the white
> racists run their international con game on the suffering peoples. We have been
> brainwashed to believe that we are powerless and that there is nothing we can
> do for ourselves to bring about a speedy liberation for our people.[26]

The initial organizing principle behind the Black Panther Party was black self
defense against police brutality. The police, who according to Newton constituted an "occupying army" in the black ghetto, were looked upon by the Panthers as a part of the apparatus of colonialism in black America:

> We believe we can end police brutality in our black community by organizing
> black self-defense groups that are dedicated to defending our black community
> from racist police oppression and brutality. The Second Amendment to the
> Constitution of the United States gives a right to bear arms. We therefore be-

lieve that all black people should arm themselves for self defense.[27]

A comprehensive picture of the militant-radical mindset shows that, operating from an anti-imperialist framework, many black radicals and militants justified their posture of violence as one of defensive retaliatory violence. They conceptualized themselves as a colonized group, behind enemy lines, *trapped* within enemy territory. The need for self-defense against what they called the "pig" forces was seen as a practical assertion for survival.

Armed self-defense, as advocated by such militants as Robert F. Williams, was viewed as a necessity to a group under siege. Williams, the chapter leader of the Monroe, North Carolina NAACP, insisted that "violent resistance to savage dehumanization was justified." He too championed the right to bear arms long before the Panthers, "Equality, total equality, must grant the black citizen the same right of temper and the same right of self-defense as any other citizen."[28] The white citizen councils of the rural South would not be the only ones armed. Violence became an inevitable part of the movement.

Black militants and radicals considered themselves as "colonized individuals," and spoke from that perspective. Therefore white and black radicalism during the 1960s would not be synonymous. H. Rap Brown, as did Fanon, came to believe that racism was integral to the maintenance of colonialism and that poor oppressed whites in fact form "a part of the colonizing force," and declared that "some of the most racist whites are the oppressed whites."[29] Although the Party did embrace the White Left, Huey Newton considered that Black Americans in general were colonized, claiming, "The Black Panthers Party's position is that the Black people in the country are definitely colonized, and suffer from the colonial plight more than any ethnic group. As far as blacks are concerned, of course, we're at the very bottom of this ladder, we're exploited not only by the small group of ruling class, we're oppressed, and repressed by even working class whites."[30]

The Black Power movement came to ultimately express the need for black solidarity and black self-determinism. And this is why workers in the Deep South, fueled by the inflammatory diatribes of Malcolm X, and other black activists in SNCC and CORE, began to identify with the position of the "colonized" amid daily harassment, and humiliation.. By the summer of 1964, there were calls that the SNCC "must be black lead." Whites came to be considered the enemy, while many of the black organizers in both groups began to consider themselves under siege. Huey P. Newton went so far as to characterize all black inmates as "prisoners of war."

If workers in SNCC and CORE were subject to daily and often times harsh indiscriminate violence, the arduous task of fighting for freedom sometimes took a considerable psychological and physical toll. Violent action during the Selma Campaign alone yielded three deaths, as in the Freedom Summer the prior year. The black psychiatrist Alvin Poussaint, who traveled with SNCC during the Freedom Summer of 1964, described the apparent increasingly aggressive anger of many SNCC workers as a bid for "psychological emancipa-

tion" through vigorous and vocal assertive self-determinism.[31] Doubts over the
ability of peaceful actions to successfully achieve the movement's objectives,
along with a growing desire for vengeful physical retaliation, began to emerge.
The physically violent reactions taken by white authority figures in dealing with
peacefully protesting black individuals caused mental anguish among many
blacks. The shift in the movement toward aggressive expression, on the part of
the radicals and militants, was also explained by Pouissant as integral to the
movement for black self identity:

> Through systematic oppression aimed at extinguishing his aggressive drive, the
> black American has been effectively castrated and rendered abjectly compliant
> by white America. Since appropriate rage at such emasculation could be ex-
> pressed directly only the at great risk, the Negro repressed and suppressed it,
> but only at great cost to his psychic development. Today his "aggression rage"
> constellation, rather than self hatred, appears to be at the core of the Negro's
> social and psychological difficulties.[32]

A tendency toward self-hatred produced by the suppression of the black self was
working in tandem with this "aggressive rage constellation" in black radical
expression thus producing the hegemonic masculinities that bursts forth from the
coalition within the context of the black power discourse.

The American Civil Rights Movement was simply *not* a non-violent revolution. Along the trail of nearly every major campaign, from Albany through Birmingham and Selma, violence followed the movement. The violence of enraged
white extremists was often answered by rioting black insurgents. Philosophical
non-violence and direct action were virtually anathema to the already insurgent
rural black masses. The renegade Deacons for Self-Defense, established in Jons-
boro, Louisiana in 1964, saw themselves as the staunch protectors of various
civil rights workers. Comprised of mostly middle aged black veterans of WWII
and the Korean Conflict, the Deacons regularly carried firearms, communicated
through CB radios and walkie talkies to "coordinate their movements," and pa-
trolled the offices of SNCC and CORE workers.[33] As well, many civil rights
workers felt the need to carry personal firearms. In one of his final interviews
with *Essence* magazine, Stokely Carmichael tells us he carried a 38 caliber re-
volver.[34]

The guerrilla warfare fantasy was connected to the violence or retaliatory
violence that came with the movement. But it remained that, simply a rhetorical
fantasy. There was no massive organized movement to overthrow the American
government or to "burn the town down." The violent confrontations instigated
by some Black Power advocates, within the militant-radical mindset, were seen
as defensive retaliation and justified. As the Black Studies scholar William
L.Van Deburg asserted, the fear of a black insurrection was very real for many
white Americans, although it was hysterical and ultimately unfounded, "Terri-
fied whites conjured up visions of campus radicals, Muslim separatists, and
black teenage gang members banded together in an unholy pact to kill whitey or

force him to his knees."[35]

Although we find an affirmation of "absolute violence" and the notion that de colonization is "always a violent phenomena" within Frantz Fanon's *The Wretched of the Earth*, many black radicals and militants, who aligned themselves with the plight of the Third World, saw their actions within the scope of retaliatory violence only. In his book *Revolutionary Suicide*, Huey P. Newton considered the initial posture of violence adopted by the Black Panther Party a "necessary" and cathartic phase. In his speech, given ten months before his death in 1965, "The Black Revolution" Malcolm X continued to cultivate the notion of retaliatory violence, "It won't be blood that's going to flow only on one side. . . . If there is to be bleeding, it should be reciprocal—bleeding on both sides;" Malcolm went on to state within this same speech that the black man was "within his rights," as the victim of brutality in the pursuit of his rights, "to do whatever necessary to protect himself."[36]

The violence instigated by the militants and radicals was primarily on the defensive, rather than a cohesive and well organized offensive. The guerrilla warfare fantasy remained more a rhetorical allusion than a well thought out plan of action. The very diversity of Black Power ideologies lends itself to the idea that there was not enough cohesion within the Black Power movement to surmount a massive attack on the American government. Malcolm X, through his transformation, continued to believe in the right to bear arms as a defensive tactic, "we assert the Afro-American right of self defense. The Constitution of the USA clearly reaffirms the right of every American citizen to bear arms. And as Americans, we will not give up a single right."[37]

Malcolm X was actively courted by black activists within the movement before his assassination in 1965. He debated Floyd Mckissick in the 1950s, and went to Birmingham in 1963 and to Selma in 1965. Many black radicals and militants used the symbol of Malcolm X as a point of reference. In his now famous eulogy of the slain leader, the actor Ozzie Davis called Malcolm a "shinning black prince." Milton Henry, a Yale educated lawyer, traveled with Malcolm X to Africa in 1964. Henry and his brother Richard, having dropped their "slave names," formed the Republic of New Africa in 1967 as a secular version of the Nation of Islam. They were territorial separatists interested in securing land or a black nation state to be erected across the Southern United States:

> There is, fortunately, a civilized rule of land possession. It says that if a people have lived on a land traditionally, if they have worked and developed it, and if they have fought to stay there, that land is theirs. It is upon this rule of international law that Africans in America rest their claim for land—in America. We have lived for over 300 years in the so-called Black Belt, we have worked and developed the land and we have fought to stay there.[38]

Bobby Seale was convinced that Malcolm X "was his rebellion." If so, he was also the rebellion of Stokely Carmichael, H. Rap Brown, and Huey P. Newton who said:

Malcolm was my personal friend. My leader. My unknown partner. Malcolm's
rebellion was mine and Steve's. I was wishing I could talk like Malcolm X,
think like him . . . they Can't kill my leader![39]

Speaking to a crowd of some 500 during the Selma campaign, one week before
his death, Malcolm X admonished his audience, "The white man should thank
God that Dr. King is holding his people in check, because there are others who
don't feel that way. And there are other ways to obtain their ends."[40] As the in-
vited guest of SNCC in December 1964, speaking to a group of McComb, Mississippi youth, at the Hotel Theresa in Harlem, Malcolm X commented on non-
violence:

> I don't go along with any kind of nonviolence unless everybody's going to be
> nonviolent. If they make the Ku Klux Klan nonviolent, I'll be nonviolent. If
> they make the White Citizens Council nonviolent, I'll be nonviolent. But as
> long as you've got somebody else not being nonviolent, I don't want anybody
> coming to me talking any nonviolent talk. I don't think it is fair to tell our peo-
> ple to be nonviolent unless someone is out there making the Klan and the Citi-
> zens Council and these other groups also be nonviolent.[41]

For Malcolm X, there was a certain veneer of indignity to non-violent direct
action. And he had a profound influence upon those who heard him speak.
    El-Hajj Malik El-Shabazz thought, perhaps, the devil was not white; he was
no longer Malcolm. Malcolm X worshipped at the Ka'ba, the most sacred shrine
of Islam, and prayed with Muslims who had eyes that were "the bluest of the
blue." A transformation had occurred, "In the words and the in the actions and in
the deeds of the white Muslims, I felt the same sincerity that I felt among the
black African Muslims of Nigeria, Sudan, and Ghana. We were truly all the
same brothers," states Malcolm X of his time in Mecca.[42] Although a transformation did occur, Malcolm X was no less aware of the African American plight
and no less an advocate of retaliatory violence as he told his young guests at the
Theresa Hotel two months before his death:

> You've got to know that you've got as much power on your side as that Ku
> Klux Klan has on its side. And when you know that you've got as much power
> on your ideas the Klan has on its side, you'll talk the same kind of language
> with that Klan as the Klan is talking with you . . . it's time for us to organize
> and band together and equip ourselves and qualify ourselves. And once you can
> protect yourself, you don't have to worry about being hurt.[43]

Malcolm X, in essence, told his young audience, attended by SNCC, that it was
acceptable to use the term "black power." What Malcolm failed to tell his young
disciples, was that things would become more dangerous and someone would
have to die. Roy Wilkins had admonished the new radicals and militants when
he cautioned them not to attempt to use power "they didn't already have."

Someone should have also warned them that, "You can't say Black Power!"

Notes

1 Alex Haley, and Malcolm X, *The Autobiography of Malcolm X.* (1965; New York: Balantine Books, 1993), 256.

2 William L. Van Deburg, *New Day in Babylon: the Black Power Movement and American Culture, 1965-1975* (Chicago and London: University of Chicago Press, 1992), 2.

3 Amiri Baraka, "Malcolm as Ideology," in *Malcolm in Our Own Image*, ed. Joe Wood (New York, 1992) 29.

4 Phillis Wheatley, "To the Right Honorable William, Earl of Dartmouth," in *The Black Poets*, ed. Dudley Randall (New York: Bantam Books, 1971), 38.

5 Claude Mckay, "The Negro's Tragedy," in *The Black Poets*, ed. Dudley Randall, (New York: Bantam Books, 1971), 63.

6 Nikki Giovanni, "This Poem Hates," in *Blues For All The Changes* (New York: William Morrow and Company, 1999), 20.

7 James Turner, "The Sociology of Black Nationalism," *Black Scholar* (December 1969): 18-27.

8 Ibid.

9 The current remnants of Elijah Muhammad's conglomerate include the Lost Found Nation of Islam lead by Silas Muhammad and Abu Koss, Brother Solomon and Aboss Rassoull's group the United Nation of Islam based in Camp Springs, Maryland, John Muhammad's Nation of Islam Temple in Detroit, Wallace Muhammad's more than 200 masjids once known as the World Community of Islam, and Louis Farrakhan's NOI.

10 Ernest Allen, Jr., "Religious Heterodoxy and Nationalist Tradition: The Continuing Evolution of the Nation of Islam," *Black Scholar* 26 (Fall/Winter 1996): 36.

11 Edward G. Rogoff, "Perhaps the Times Have Not Caught Up to Marcus Garvey, An Early Champion of Ethnic Entrepreneurship," *Journal of Small Business Management* 36 (July 1998): 66-72.

12 Ernest Allen, Jr., "Religious Heterodoxy and Nationalist Tradition: The Continuing Evolution of the Nation of Islam," *Black Scholar* 26 (Fall/Winter 1996): 2-35. By the 1970s, the NOI had accumulated a significant amount of assets including 14.5 million dollars in Chicago property which included bakeries, cleaners, and a supermarket along with a 22 million dollar fish import business.

13 Ibid.

14 Alex Haley and Malcolm X, *The Autobiography of Malcolm X.* (1964; New York: Balantine Books, 1993), 251.

15 Malcolm X and James Farmer, "Separation or Integration," in *Black Protest Thought in the Twentieth Century*, ed. August Meier, (Indianapolis and New York: The Bobbs Merrill Company, 1971), 392-393.

16 John T. McCartney, *Black Power Ideologies: An Essay in African American Political Thought* (Philadelphia: Temple University Press, 1982), 175-176.

17 Mckissick's Soul City, a 2,500 acre black model city supported by black enterprise in North Carolina, gave the impression that his pluralism was indeed bisected by remnants of the separatist impulse.

18 Huey P. Newton, "To the Black Movement," in *To Die For the People,* ed. Toni Morrison, (New York: Writers and Readers Publishers, 1973), 92.

19 Alex Haley and Malcolm X, *The Autobiography of Malcolm X.* (1964; New York: Balantine Books, 1993), 252.

20 Malcolm X, and James Farmer, "Separation or Integration," in *Black Protest Thought in The Twentieth Century,* ed. August Meier, (Indianapolis and New York: The Bobbs Merrill Company, 1971), 390.

21 Ibid.

22 During his tenure as national spokesman for the Nation, Malcolm was responsible for almost single handedly increasing the membership of the organization to more than 40,000 converts.

23 Malcolm X, "The Ballot or the Bullet," in *Malcolm X Speaks,* ed. George Brietman, (New York: Grove/Atlantic Inc., 1965), 26.

24 Franz Fanon, "From Concerning Violence," in *Modern Black Nationalism from Marcus Garvey to Louis Farrakhan,* ed. William L. Van De Burg, (New York: New York University Press, 1997), 130-131.

25 H. Rap Brown, *Die, Nigger, Die!* (New York: Dial Press, 1969), 125.

26 Huey P. Newton, "In Defense of Self-Defense I," in *To Die for the People.* ed. Toni Morrison, (1973; New York: Writers and Readers Publishers, 1995), 83.

27 Huey P. Newton, and Bobby Seale, "Black Panther Party Platform and Program: What We Want, What We Believe," *The Black Panther*, November 16, 1968, 23.

28 Robert F. Williams, "For Effective Self Defense," in *Black Protest Thought in the Twentieth Century*, ed. August Meier, (New York: The Bobbs Merrill Company, 1971), 364.

29 Brown, in *Die, Nigger, Die!*, 125.

30 Huey P. Newton, "To the RNA," in *The Black Panthers Speak*, ed. Philip S. Foner, (1970; New York: DA Capo Press, 1995), 71.

31 Alvin Poussaint, "How the White Problem Spawned Black Power," *Ebony*, August 1967, 89-92.

32 Alvin Poussaint, "A Negro Psychiatrist Explains the Negro Psyche," *New York Times* August 20, 1967, 52-53.

33 Adam Fairclough, *Race and Democracy: The Civil Rights Struggle in Louisiana, 1915 - 1972* (Athens and London: University of Georgia Press, 1995), 342.

34 Isabel Wilkerson, "Soul Survivor: From Stokely Carmichael to Kwame Ture, Still Ready for the Revolution," *Essence,* May 1998, 109 - 190.

35 William L. Van Deburg, *New Day in Babylon: The Black Power Movement And American Culture.* (Chicago and London: University of Chicago Press, 1992), 167.

36 Malcolm X, *Malcolm X Speaks,* 48.

37 Malcolm X, "Malcolm X Founds the Organization of Afro-American Unity," in *Black Protest Thought in The Twentieth Century*, ed. August Meier, (New York: The Bobbs Merrill Company, 1971), 415.

38 Imari Abubakari Obadele, "The Struggle is For Land," *Black Scholar,* (February 1972): 25.

39 Bobby Seale, *A Lonely Rage: The Autobiography of Bobby Seale* (New York:

1978) 134.

40 "Civil Rights," *The New York Times,* February 12, 1965, 16.

41 Malcolm X, in *Malcolm X Speaks,* 138-139.

42 Alex Haley, and Malcolm X, *The Autobiography of Malcolm X,* (New York: Balantine Books, 1993), 347.

43 Malcolm X, in *Malcolm X Speaks*, 143-145.

Chapter 4

You Can't Say Black Power!

A spectre is haunting America
the spectre of hoodooism…

Ishmael Reed, "Black Power Poem"

The radical cadre of the Student Nonviolent Coordinating Committee and the Congress of Racial Equality found that there was a necessity to say "black power" in 1966. Malcolm X said they could. It was Roy Wilkins who warned them that, "You Can't Say Black Power!" Integration was the goal of the NAACP, according to Wilkins, and to associate black with power implied altogether something else. Many in the coalition denounced the slogan as connotatively incendiary because of the potential response it would evoke from white people. Black radicals believed that aggressive expression was an essential facet of racial solidarity and black self-determinism. Dr. Alvin Poussaint's, aforementioned, theory of the "aggressive rage constellation" was in evidence here. It was a part of the power to say "Black Power!" Floyd McKissick maintained that black people had to say "black power" in the "affirmative," and to "white peoples faces," in order "to be adult and to stop living a lie."[1] Stokely Carmichael characterized the initial debate over the slogan in such a way:

> Now we are engaged in a psychological struggle in this country and that struggle is whether or not black people have the right to use the words they want to use without white people giving their sanction to it. We maintain, whether they like it or not, we gon' use the word "black power" and let them address themselves to that. We are not gonna wait for white people to sanction black power. We're tired of waiting. Every time black people move in this country, they're forced to defend their position before they moved.[2]

SNCC and CORE were pushed to the radical extreme long before the phrase "Black Power" was ever uttered. The debate was larger than the term.

When the radicals of SNCC and CORE became fixated on a slogan "without program,"[3] Martin Luther King, Jr. moved closer to the pluralism they cultivated. King became, seemingly, enamored by the idea that perhaps an independent black organization could lead to integration. The radicals of SNCC and CORE became convinced that separation seemed more plausible. They subsequently sacrificed coalition ties for the new ideology of "Black Power." This

was an ideology that they were never completely able to define. The Freedom
Rides, coupled with their journey through the Deep South and the Freedom
Summer Project of 1964, led both organizations to a embrace the idea of inde-
pendent black organization.

The Congress of Racial Equality (CORE) began as an outgrowth of the
Christian student pacifist movement of the 1930s. Its members revolutionized
the practices of direct-action challenges against segregation throughout the cities
of the North. CORE members were influenced by the ideas of late nineteenth
century progressivism and the social gospel of Washington Gladdens and Walter
Rauschenbush. This was not unlike the source of Martin Luther King's philosophical base in non-violence and social reform. The seminary students who
formed the first chapter of CORE in Chicago, Illinois in 1941 held a firm belief
that Christian ethics could be applied to contemporary social reform.[4] They also
believed that society could be transformed through a planned campaign of nonviolent direct action. Nearly twenty years before the first "sit-in," there was a
"sit-down" staged by CORE in Chicago.

On February 1, 1960 four black students from the North Carolina Agricul-
tural and Technical College staged a sit-in at an F.W. Woolworth lunch counter
located in downtown Greensboro, North Carolina. By the end of the week the
"sit-ins" spread into communities beyond Greensboro. By the end of the month
more than twenty communities, in seven states across the American South, had
demonstrators who were "sitting in." Sympathy boycotts began in the North as
well. Some CORE affiliates were instrumental in these boycotts. In April of this
same year, while the protests had gone from four to more than 50,000 participants nation wide, an organizing conference to formerly establish the Student
Non-Violent Coordinating Committee took place through the instigation of Ella
Baker of SCLC.[5] The students came together at Shaw University in Raleigh,
North Carolina on the weekend of April 15. They represented some 56 schools
from 58 Southern communities across the American south including an estimated 126 student delegates present.[6] The majority of these students were African American, as was the composition of SNCC.

Izell Blair, Joseph McNeil, Franklin McCain, and David Richmond set the
flame for the largest black protest movement in American history. Their concern
to change the status quo at the lunch counter evolved into a movement to over-
turn segregation. Their concerns were similar to the young divinity students
clustered around the University of Chicago who sought to challenge segregation
in northern cities. James Farmer, George Houser, Bernice Fisher, Homer Jack,
Joe Guinn, and James R. Robinson were the most instrumental in creating the
organization known as CORE. Using the techniques of Ghandhi, CORE's foundation was grounded in a philosophy of non-violence and interracial harmony.
Four of the founding members were white and two were African American.

The Congress of Racial Equality challenged segregation in residential housing, restaurants, and places of public recreation. In 1942 they established the co-
opt Fellowship House to combat residential segregation, and in 1943 a series of

"sit-downs" were staged at facilities across downtown Chicago. The integrated "Journey of Reconciliation" of 1947 was embarked upon to test compliance in interstate travel across the Upper South.[7] By the end of the decade, CORE had more than fifteen affiliates across the nation in cities such as Los Angeles, Detroit, and New York. In the 1950s, CORE experienced a decline due to financing, national continuity, internal conflict, and the sphere of McCarthyism. With no concrete footholds in the South, the Civil Rights era of the 1960s was ushered in by the insurgence of the Southern Christian Leadership Conference, the National Association for the Advancement of Colored People, and the Student Nonviolent Coordinating Committee.

Both organizations were introduced to the Deep South by way of the Freedom Rides in 1961. The forty-one year old James Farmer, one of the divinity students most instrumental in forming CORE in 1941, who had recently become the group's National Director, rose to the stature of Martin Luther King, Jr. during this journey. He was the architect of the Freedom Rides. With the Freedom Rides, CORE became an integral part of the coalition along with SNCC. This ride into the Deep South strengthened SNCC, and reinvigorated CORE. Many floundering chapters of CORE, located throughout the South, became reinvigorated. The Freedom Rides placed both groups at the forefront of the coalition, especially within rural black communities in the Deep South.

The Freedom Rides began in early May 1961 to emulate the "Journey" of 1947, and to specifically test compliance with the Supreme Court ruling in *Boynton v. Virginia* delivered in December 1960. This decision prohibited segregation within busing terminals and facilities. It was an echo of the *Morgan* case which banned segregation in interstate travel in 1946.

The journey of 1961 began with CORE and ended with SNCC in Jackson, Mississippi. As they did in 1947, a group of integrated riders departed from a Trailways bus terminal in Washington, D. C. James Farmer was with them. Through Virginia and North Carolina, the riders survived their passage virtually unscathed, but in Rock Hill, South Carolina they were viciously assaulted by angry white mobs at a Greyhound terminal. The further South they went, the harsher the ride became. In Atlanta they endured "closed" facilities on May 13, and on the outskirts of Birmingham, Alabama on May 14 a fire bomb exploded in one bus and several participants were severely injured. On May 17, CORE called for a brief suspension of the rides. The SNCC activists, undaunted by this incident, boarded buses and continued south. The participants were led by John Lewis, a young seminary student from Nashville, Tennessee. Another young college student, born in Trinidad and raised in New York, named Stokely Carmichael joined the fray as well.

With a vow to continue the ride into Jackson, Mississippi a temporary alliance was formed between SNCC, CORE, and SCLC under the guise of the Freedom Ride Coordinating Committee. The goal of this alliance was to "fill the jails." The contentious journey into the heart of the South ended for many at Mississippi's Parchman Penitentiary. Freedom rider Fred Leonard described the circumstances as the contingent entered Mississippi:

> When we got to Jackson, we didn't see anybody except the police. We never
> got stopped. They passed us right through the white terminal, into the paddy
> wagon, and into jail. There was no violence in Mississippi. The next day, we
> went to court. The prosecutor got up, accused us of trespassing, took his seat.
> Our attorney, Jack Young, got up to defend us. . . . While he was defending us,
> the judge turned his back, looked at the wall. When he finished, the judge
> turned around—*bam*, sixty days in the state penitentiary—and there we were,
> on the way to Parchman, maximum security.[8]

Fred Leonard also spoke of the psychological terror imposed upon the riders as
they reached Parchman. According to Leonard, the toughest African Americans
already in the prison were used against the newly convicted protesters who refused to conform. When Fred Leonard refused "to conform," by refusing to give
up his mattress, this is what happened:

> Everybody was peaceful, and let their mattress go, but I remembered the night
> before, when I had to sleep on that steel. So they came in to take my mattress. I
> was holding my mattress. They drug me out into the cellblock. I still had my
> mattress, I wouldn't turn it loose. They were using black inmates to come and
> get our mattresses, and I mean the *inmates*. And there was this guy, Peewee
> they called him, short and muscular. They said, "Peewee get him." Peewee
> came down on my head. *Whomp, whomp*—he was crying. Peewee was crying.
> And I still had my mattress. . . . It hurt Peewee more than it hurt me . . . they
> had these things   they put on my wrists like handcuffs, and they started twist-
> ing and tightening them up—my bones start cracking and going on and finally I
> turned my mattress loose.[9]

James Farmer was at Parchman with the other riders and this gave his organization the national spotlight for a time.

"The Freedom Rides solved the interstate transportation issue," state August
Meier and Elliot Rudwick in their book *CORE: A Study in the Civil Rights
Movement*. On September 22, 1961 the Interstate Commerce Commission issued
an order that banned segregation in busing terminals and facilities thereby bol-
stering the *Boynton* decision. It seemed as if one problem was finally solved.
But there were other concerns to attend to, such as voter education and registration, a far more pressing problem in the Deep South. The Freedom Rides allowed the activists of SNCC and CORE to foster strong footholds across the
Southern United States. Many who came by bus remained.

Protestors came to communities such as Plaquemine, Louisiana, McComb,
Mississippi, Lowdes, Alabama, and Albany, Georgia. The Harlem born activist,
and Harvard graduate of philosophy and mathematical logic, Bob Moses first
came to McComb in the summer of 1961 to establish a voter registration drive.
He was eventually joined by others from SNCC. Charles Sherrod and Cordell
Reagan, veterans of the Freedom Rides, went to Albany, Georgia in the Fall of

1961 in service for SNCC. The thirty three year old school teacher James Forman became the Executive Director of SNCC in the fall of 1961. Stokely Carmichael went to Alabama. CORE created, revived, and maintained several new chapters throughout the South in such places as New Orleans, Louisiana. Floyd B. McKissick, a former lawyer for the NAACP in the 1950s, and leader of the North Carolina sit-in movement in Durham, became National Chairman for CORE during this period.

The four southern states which felt the greatest presence of SNCC and CORE were Louisiana, Mississippi, Alabama and Georgia. SNCC's national headquarters was in Atlanta, Georgia. The Council of Federated Organizations (COFO) was created specifically to coordinate efforts among these two groups in Mississippi along with the NAACP in 1962. Once the activists of SNCC and CORE realized the severity of the situation for blacks in the south, they broadened their perspective to encompass political as well as economic power for the locals. Amid daily harassment and facing death at nearly every turn, it was not hard for many within the ranks to begin to conceptualize themselves as being a part of the Third World. They found that the parameters of the movement had to shift beyond public accommodation and voting rights, as they met the political and economic conditions that were the "Third World" of the rural black South. The pre-conditions of the Black Revolution were set by SNCC and CORE in the Deep South. Between the years of 1964 and 1966, these two groups made the transition from integration, to political pluralism, into the depths of racial separatism.

When the members of SNCC and CORE reached the center of the Deep South, they became intimately aware of the broader struggle for civil rights. Many were pushed to the limit. Bob Moses, architect of the Freedom Summer project, became unraveled after nearly four years in Mississippi. The atmosphere of blatant hostility produced campaigns of terror which resulted in the serious injury and death of several civil rights workers and volunteers. Medger Evers lost the struggle in Mississippi of 1963; Michael Schwerner, James Chaney and Andrew Goodman lost the fight in Philadelphia, Mississippi of 1964. Jimmy Lee Jackson and James Reeb both fell victim in the Selma, Alabama campaign of 1965.

As the movement became more violent, the actions of SNCC and CORE became more aggressive. If the workers in both organizations encountered a resurgent Klu Klux Klan, they also met an already insurgent contingent of rural blacks. It was Stokely Carmichael's contention that nonviolence should remain more a tactic than a principle for many in SNCC who could abandon the tactic when necessary:

> Most of us in SNCC did not accept nonviolence as a principle. We saw it as a tactic. As a principle, you have to use it all the time under all conditions. As a tactic, we could use it today if it was working fine. If it wasn't working, tomorrow we could toss hand grenades.[10]

In his book *Let the Trumpet Sound: A Life of Martin Luther King, Jr.*, Stephen B. Oates suggests that the black section of Montgomery was ready to riot before they were ready to march in December of 1955. Gloria Styles, a veteran of the Albany Campaign of 1961-1962, has stated that SNCC was "never nonviolent" when they came to her town.[11] The culture of violence remained as an integral part of both black and white rural southern communities throughout the movement. Through periodic campaigns of terror, blacks were kept in their place, but not all were resigned to their fate:

> CORE workers soon discovered, moreover, that many ordinary blacks regarded strict nonviolence as nonsensical. In rural Louisiana the ownership of guns was commonplace, and here, where blacks were isolated and most vulnerable, guns were often seen as the only deterrent to white violence. In East Carroll Parish John Henry Scott dusted off his shot gun and began target practice. . . . In West Feliciana, CORE workers were only too glad to see black men bring weapons to their voter registration clinics.[12]

Blacks of the rural Deep South, after years of a protracted struggle, began to see armed defense as a logical necessity. The Deacons for Defense and Justice, a group of gun-toting middle aged black Korean War veterans, served as the staunch protectors of CORE workers in Louisiana, and SNCC workers in Mississippi.

CORE conducted efforts primarily in Louisiana in such places as New Orleans, Bogalusa, and Jonesboro, while SNCC made a concentrated effort to reconstruct Mississippi in such places as Jackson, McComb, and Meridian. The quest for Mississippi was perhaps the bloodiest and most strenuous battle. One outgrowth from the battle for the Deep South was a commitment to independent black organization. This brought the lead articulators of "Black Power" into immediate conflict with the moderate wing at Selma. The lead articulators of "Black Power," Stokely Carmichael and James Forman of the SNCC and Floyd Mckissick of CORE emerged directly out of this struggle in the Deep South.

Orchestrated by Bob Moses of SNCC, the Mississippi Summer project of 1964 was to be a most ambitious plan to reform the South. Mississippi was the first major example. According to John Lewis, it was a plan to "bring the nation to Mississippi." The challenge for Mississippi produced, first the "parallel" political organization known as the Mississippi Freedom Democrats. Then the Freedom Summer Project of 1964 fostered a commitment to independent black organization that only intensified at Lowndes County, Alabama in1965. The struggle for Mississippi also produced the James Meredith March Against Fear in 1966.

The tensions of Freedom Summer were recognized by Moses before the 1964 Democratic National Convention. For the SNCC, the decision to surmount a fully *integrated* assault on Mississippi was debated as recognized by Bob

Moses:

> What was in the offing was whether SNCC could integrate itself,
> as it were, and live   as a sort of island of integration in a sea of separa-
> tion. And SNCC was trying to work itself out as an organization which was
> integrated in all levels. The question of white volunteers, or white SNCC
> staffers, came up in this context. Are they to be confined to the Atlanta office?
> And they're pushing, those that are there, to get out in the field? There was
> constant pressure about what the goals of the organization were.[13]

Stokely Carmichael, like Moses, questioned the role of whites in the movement.
He was concerned with white leadership in the movement, because of its implications upon black civil rights workers, contending that it served to further foster an "inferiority" complex already prevalent within the black community.[14]

The African American psychiatrist Alvin Poussaint, then Field Director of
the Medical Committee for Human Rights in Jackson, Mississippi and professor
of psychiatry at Tufts University Medical College in Boston, observed the same
tensions between black and white civil rights workers as well. He observed that
many black workers began to view their white counterparts as provocative inter-
lopers and as "hangers-on" in their cause. Poussaint went saw far as to describe
these contentious relations as being "fraught with severe social and psychological difficulties" caused by the reality of racism in America:

> They had learned painfully that the realities of racism had affected their minds
> in so many ways that normal human relations between the races was fraught
> with severe social and psychological difficulties. . . . What I found was that
> most of them felt that white civil rights volunteers caused too many problems
> which at that time seemed irresolvable. They also felt that most of the whites
> who came down were either just white racists of another variety or that they
> had psychological "hang-ups" centered around black people. In most cases,
> they were able to present evidence from their personal experience to support
> their switch from a desire for an "integrated movement" to an "all-black move-
> ment."[15]

The mere presence of white involvement in the movement, on a large scale, as
reflected in the Mississippi Summer Project, made black workers excruciatingly
aware of their own "inferior" place within American society.

According to the observations of Poussaint, this black "inferiority complex"
was significantly reinforced by a large white presence within the midst of the
black community. One of the black workers that conversed with Poussaint
stated, "I feel that they should go and try to help their folks and stay away from
the black community because all they're doing is screwing up the minds of the
local people."[16] Many of the black civil rights workers that spoke with Poussaint
were in fact literally afraid that the provocative actions taken by the whites
could get them killed once the whites left. The introduction of a significant

amount of white involvement in the movement changed the entire composition of the cause to many blacks.[17]

If whites felt the intimidation of blacks amongst them, a fear that is historically documented, Poussaint asserts that there was a tremendous amount of intimidation and anxiety felt by blacks in the presence of whites within the movement. This feeling of intimidation, or inferiority, can be found in the justifications for "Black Power" that emerged from SNCC after the 1964 Freedom Summer Project. It was in fact the crux of SNCC position paper concerning Black Power, "Blacks, in fact, feel intimidated by the presence of whites, because of their knowledge of the power that whites have over their lives. One white person can come into a meeting of black people and change the complexion of that meeting."[18] Within this same paper, the advocates of Black Power from SNCC asserted that, "If people must express themselves freely, there has to be a climate in which they can do this." Therefore, because the presence of whites was an intimidating force, "a climate has to be created whereby blacks can express themselves." This climate would be fostered within an entirely black political organization.

Bob Moses, having spent nearly four years in Mississippi, formed a plan to challenge the legitimacy of the existing political order in Mississippi during the spring of 1964. This plan was the establishment of the Mississippi Freedom Democratic Party (MFDP). By maneuvering, or adapting, through the system power could be had. The MFDP was set up specifically as a parallel structure, within the system, to empower the local black people:

> The Mississippi Freedom Democratic Party was founded April 26, 1964 in order to create an opportunity for meaningful political expression for the 438, 000 adult Negro Mississippians who traditionally have been denied this right. In addition to being a political instrument, the FDP provides a focus for the coordination of civil rights activity in the state and around the country. Although its members do not necessarily think in these terms, the MFDP is the organization above all others whose work is most directly forcing a realignment within the Democratic Party. . . . All individuals and organizations who have an interest in the destruction of the Dixiecrat-Republican alliance and the purging of the racists from the Democratic Party are potential allies of the MFDP.[19]

It was this pluralist approach to power which brought the challenge for Mississippi to the national level. Under the leadership of Moses through the summer of 1964, SNCC managed to expand their activity into all five of Mississippi's congressional districts in collaboration with CORE through the Council of Confederated Organizations [COFO].

The pluralist approach to empowerment gathered steam throughout the summer of 1964, as the Freedom Summer project was implemented. The leaders of the MFDP began to create a structure "at all levels" to the regular Mississippi Democratic delegation. A state executive committee of twelve was created and the Freedom Democrats went on to register several thousand voters. But despite

these gallant efforts, candidates chosen by the Freedom Democrats were de-
feated in the summer's primaries and were subsequently barred space on the
ballot, as independents, by the Mississippi State Board of Election:

> Because the Freedom Democrats were barred from the "regular" organ-
> ization, they set up a parallel structure at all levels, including having
> their own system of voter registration. Simplified registration forms
> and procedures based on those used in several northern states were
> adopted.[20]

Despite great strides being made in voter registration, the MFDP did not accomplish its goal to defeat the regular Democrats in Mississippi. Their plight was
then taken up at the 1964 Democratic National Convention in Atlantic City
where they proceeded to challenge the legitimacy of the Dixiecrat stronghold
over the Deep South:

> It was at this point [having been barred from the ballot as independents] that the
> MFDP reorganized itself to conduct a mock election and to challenge the cre-
> dentials of the Mississippi delegation to the Democratic National Convention.
> During the week of July, 1964 precinct meetings were held in 26 Mississippi
> counties as alternatives to the "regular" Democratic precinct meetings which
> barred Negroes. An estimated 3, 500 persons attended these meetings. At the
> end of July, county conventions were held in 35 counties as part of the policy
> of structuring the MFDP in a fashion parallel to that of the "regular" Democ-
> rats.[21]

Through adaptation, the Mississippi Freedom Democratic Party attempted to
work within the system by creating a parallel structure. It did not work. Only
two Freedom Democrats were allowed seats on the floor at the convention in
Atlantic City, one black and one white. The MFDP was an integrated organization. The "compromise" offered by the Democratic Party to seat the two Freedom Democrats, alongside the regular Mississippi delegation, was ultimately
rejected. Although the Freedom Democrats managed to force their way onto the
floor to occupy many of the seats vacated by regular Democrats, by using passes
from adjacent delegations, the convention challenge was seen as a defeat by the
SNCC. They had come to *unseat* the regulars, not for compromise as one SNCC
observer insisted:

> We would prove that the MFDP's delegates were more loyal to the stated goals
> of the national party than the states' regular delegation and, therefore, deserved
> to be seated in its place. . . . Our ultimate goal was the destruction of the awe-
> some power of the Dixiecrats, who controlled over 75 percent of the most im-
> portant committees in Congress. With the Dixiecrats deposed, the way would
> have been clear for a wide ranging redistribution of wealth, power and priori-
> ties throughout the nation. This strategy, which to a large extent was the brain-
> child of Bob Moses, could have proven successful if, and only if, the leaders of

the national party had been willing to support the MFDP challenge. As it was, they ignored principle and offered the MFDP delegates a compromise—two nonvoting seats beside the regular delegation.[22]

It was the contention of Cleveland Sellers that the defeat at the national convention set the organization and the coalition on the path of no return. Sellers contended that, "things would never be the same. We left Atlantic City with the knowledge that the movement had turned into something else."[23]

Through 1966, SNCC made the transition from integration to separation. SNCC and CORE both moved from fragile unity at Selma, to independent black organizations at Lowndes, and eventually separation after the James Meredith March Against Fear at Greenwood, Mississippi in 1966. The life and death of SNCC ebbed and flowed with that of the coalition. By the end of 1964, and into the spring of 1965, SNCC had experienced a great level of growth and change. It became an organization that went from 60 full time staff members, with an annual budget of $20,000, to an organization of more than 200 professional staffers and volunteers with an annual budget of $800,000.[24] Between the years of 1964 and 1966, the civil rights coalition endured its greatest achievements with the passage of the Civil Rights Act of 1964 and the Voting Rights Act of 1965.

This was not enough for those within SNCC and CORE. With the gains of 1964 and 1965, it was the assessment of A. Philip Randolph that the civil rights movement was "caught up in a crisis of victory; a crisis which may involve great opportunity or great danger to its future fulfillment."[25] The crisis of which Randolph spoke ultimately severed the coalition.

John Lewis recognized the mood swing in SNCC during the Selma campaign:

> Anarchy and Chaos. Freedom and openness. It's amazing how one set of values can slide almost imperceptibly into another, how principles that are treasured at one moment as positive and healthy can, with time and a shift in circumstances, become forces of destruction and divisiveness. That was what had happened to SNCC by the fall of 1964. The precepts that had been so fundamental to us when we began—decentralization, minimal structure, a distrust of leadership— were now beginning to tear us apart. . . . I knew these forces were at work, that issues of SNCC's identity and its direction were being called into question. Our people were upset. They were angry. They were frustrated. But I had no idea they would move so far and so fast. . .By the time I returned SNCC was shaking at its very roots, fragmenting and threatening to fall apart under its own weight.[26]

Rift with internal strife, SNCC, unlike CORE which managed to sustain itself as an organization, fell apart with the coalition. The fragile link it held with the moderate wing of the vanguard was severed at Greenwood. With the militant hardliners pitted against the "floaters," some of the organizations most able staffers, such as John Lewis, Julian Bond, and Charles Sherrod, abandoned the group after Greenwood in 1966. Bob Moses defected from the organization in 1966. One of his co-workers Connie Curry simply said the movement "broke his heart." Cleveland Sellers was present when Robert Moses attempted to change his identity by changing his name. "I have changed my name. I will no longer be known as Robert Moses. From now on it will be Robert Parris."

> Before anyone had an opportunity to respond, he launched into a complicated existential exposition. I couldn't understand all of it. It was too heavy. He said that he was changing his name because he had been under a lot of pressure in Mississippi, that a lot of people and things were pulling at him and he wanted to cope with the situation. He said that the strain he had been under was not positive. Although Bob may have been on the verge of hysteria, he appeared to be in complete control of himself.[27]

The disillusionment of Robert Moses is an illustration of the inward disintegration of SNCC, and the end of the coalition. At the end of 1964, Moses resigned his post as director of the Council of Federated Organizations. After 1965, after briefly aligning himself with the "Atlanta Separatists," he eventually abandoned SNCC completely and moved to Tanzania.

Alabama became the focus for SNCC between 1965 and 1966, particularly in Selma, seat of Dallas County, and Lowndes County. Although SNCC had sent organizers to Selma in 1963, it was Martin Luther King, Jr. and SCLC that instigated a national voters rights campaign in January of 1965 to put pressure on the Johnson Administration to pass the Voting Rights Act. Selma was a city where the majority of the population was African American, at some 57%, according to the 1960 census. Of this majority, only 130 were registered to vote according to one Civil rights Commission report. In neighboring counties, such as Wilcox and Lowndes, there was also a large population of blacks who comprised the majority. Within these counties as well, black voter registration was primarily non-existent. Lowndes County located on the border of Dallas County had a black majority of some 80%, but not one black was registered to vote. SNCC field workers Bernard Lafayette and his wife Colia entered Selma in February of 1963 to begin a voter registration project. They were subsequently followed by SNCC organizers Worth Long, John Love, and Silas Norman. Stokely Carmichael came to Lowndes County in the spring of 1965.

Although the national voter's rights campaign in Selma 1965, which ran from January 19 through March 25, began with King and SCLC at the helm, the SNCC joined in as well. Their state headquarters were located in Dallas County. King was arrested on February 1, and the publicity garnered national attention. One month later the movement suffered its first fatality, Jimmy Lee Jackson. In response to the murder of Jackson, SCLC and SNCC came together on Sunday March 7, 1965 to lead a march from Selma to Montgomery across the Edmund Pettus Bridge. Hosea Williams of SCLC and John Lewis of SNCC preceded nearly 2,000 demonstrators across the bridge to Montgomery—directly into the clutches of Sheriff Jim Clark who unleashed a furious assault on the marchers.

The incident became known as "Bloody Sunday." The events of Bloody Sunday prompted many in the SNCC, who were previously against the march at the onset, to come to Selma in support of a continued march. Suddenly, SNCC made the decision to continue the march into Montgomery as soon as possible—after their chairman, John Lewis, had been injured in the first attempt.

Cleveland Sellers contended that the events of Bloody Sunday swayed many in the SNCC to change their mind about support for the march. Sellers also states that many in SNCC were angry and had decided that they were prepared to "ram the march down the throat of anyone who tried to stop us."[28] Under pressure from SNCC, associates in SCLC, and the U.S. Justice Department, King continued the procession to Montgomery on March 10. King, with an estimated 3,000 marchers behind him, however, suddenly made an about face away from the direction of Montgomery which lay across the bridge. This was done at the consternation SNCC participants. When the project finally continued to Montgomery, on March 25, several leading organizers from SNCC had already abandoned the plan. Parallel demonstrations by SNCC were held in surrounding areas. In demonstrations held on March 15, James Forman led 600 marchers through Montgomery. As Forman contended in his autobiography *The Making of Black Revolutionaries*, SNCC only left a semblance of individual supporters with the original march from Selma to Montgomery. SNCC as an organization, according to Forman, "generally washed our hands of the affair." The march from Selma to Montgomery was the last united stand of the coalition, as the remaining members of SNCC joined with King and SCLC, Roy Wilkins of the NAACP, and Whitney Young of the NUL across the bridge to Montgomery.

The rationale behind the Lowndes County Freedom Organization (LCFO) was similar to that of the creation of the Freedom Democrats, but it was also different. The LFCO concentrated on building a local black power base using the numerical group strength of the black majority. This organization, unlike the Mississippi Democrats, was to be all black. Utilizing the potential of the black majority base in Lowndes, the initial intention of SNCC was to "take over the county."[29] All of the candidates endorsed by the LCFO were African American. During the summer of 1966, a new consensus had emerged within SNCC. This "new consensus" managed to take over the organization as a whole. Cleveland Sellers spoke about this new consensus:

> We were also thinking black. As a matter of fact, Lowndes was the first SNCC project in which the emphasis was completely black. There was no talk about an integrated ticket for the party, which was officially known as the Lowndes County Freedom Organization (LCFO). The party's symbol, a snarling black panther, was self explanatory. We were just convinced that it was time for blacks to begin to work by themselves; to prove, once and for all, that blacks could handle black political affairs without assistance from whites.[30]

Under the careful direction of Stokely Carmichael, SNCC developed a political party and campaign with the emblem of a black panther as a mascot. There was

widespread agreement within SNCC that "it was time for SNCC to begin building independent, black organization."[31] For SNCC, it was simply an achievement to get the panther on the ballot alongside the white rooster of the regular
democrats. In Louisiana, under the direction of Ike Reynolds, CORE came to
similar conclusions.

The justification behind the LCFO was two fold. One, that *real* power was
to be had at the local level, and two, local politics controlled national politics.
This was a lesson learned after the defeat at the 1964 Democratic National Convention in Atlantic City, New Jersey that created a re-evaluation:

> it was obvious that a county-wide political organization would have little effect
> on elections for state-wide, district-wide or national office. This fact led to a re-
> evaluation of the political participation which SNCC had in the past recom-
> mended and implemented—the gubernatorial and congressional election in
> Mississippi and Alabama, the convention challenge in 1964, and certain school
> board elections in Arkansas. The re-evaluation prompted the development of
> some basic assumptions about American politics and government . . . local
> units of government are the means through which the broad national and state
> policies articulated by the U.S. government and by state governments, are im-
> plemented.[32]

The contention within SNCC was that people in such local positions as school
board officials, tax assessor, sheriff, and tax collector, were the building blocks
of power in American politics. The Lowndes County Freedom organization ran
seven candidates for various positions including sheriff and tax assessor. This
campaign was supported by a vigorous voter education and registration drive as
well. The Democratic Party of Governor George Wallace and President Lyndon
Baines Johnson, in this campaign, was labeled the party of "white supremacy."
Blacks were urged to identify with the "real" Democratic Party—the party of the
black panther rather than that of the white donkey.

Although all of the Lowndes County Freedom Organization candidates
were unsuccessful in their bids, the achievement of creating an all black party
was significant for SNCC. CORE developed a significant movement of its own
in Louisiana that was more successful than SNCC was in Alabama or Mississippi. In the 1966 November elections, eight CORE candidates were elected to
local positions. A sweet potato co-opt, organized by CORE worker John Zippert,
supported by 375 black farmers in Opalousa, Louisiana bought and developed
land to produce and sell products.

The James Meredith March Against Fear, that began on June 5, 1966,
brought SNCC and CORE together under the banner of "black power." James
Meredith's 220 mile trek of the march from Memphis, Tennessee to Jackson,
Mississippi was cut short when he was riddled with a hail of 27 pellets of buck-
shot on June 7. The coalition gathered to continue the march, but was hampered
with dissent. On June 15 Stokely Carmichael's call for an "all black march"
prompted Roy Wilkins and Whitney Young to abandon the endeavor altogether.

But the march continued with Martin Luther King, Jr. along with members of SCLC, SNCC, and CORE. In the atmosphere of which the slogan was uttered and popularized by Stokely Carmichael, one half of the coalition had taken on a new persona. The SNCC-CORE collaboration disintegrated in 1966 after Stokely Carmichael demanded, "This is the 27th time I have been arrested. I ain't going to jail no more. I ain't going to jail no more. We want Black Power!"[33]

Floyd Mckissick, who had become the National Director of CORE in March of 1966, described the atmosphere after the slogan was introduced, "Many people were disturbed because, they said, this is becoming too non-American. We're going back to our roots too much and SNCC was talking about nationalism at the time."[34] Everyone tried to define the term including those outside of the coalition in academia, the national press, and the black press. And it was also McKissick who asserted that, "In the last analysis it was a question of how Black Power would be defined . . . it was never defined."[35] Although Carmichael delivered the phrase in a volatile reactionary climate, as he was being released from jail for the twenty seventh time, John Lewis has suggested that Carmichael was swayed by the term long before Greenwood—it was a calculated risk to describe in such outwardly audacious terms the new atmosphere in SNCC which had been building since the fall of 1964.[36] Martin Luther King, Jr., in his last book *Where Do We Go From Here: Chaos or Community?,* devotes an entire chapter to the concept of Black Power, reflected upon the initial introduction of the slogan into the movement at Greenwood:

> Stokely and Floyd insisted that the slogan itself was important. "How can you arouse people to unite around a program without a slogan as a rallying cry? Didn't the labor movement have slogans? Haven't we had slogans all along in the freedom movement? What we need is a new slogan with 'black' in it." I conceded the fact that we must have slogans. But why have one that would confuse our allies, isolate the Negro community and give many prejudiced whites, who might otherwise be ashamed of their anti-Negro feeling, a ready excuse for self-justification? "Why not use the slogan 'black consciousness' or 'black equality'?" I suggested. "These phrases would be less vulnerable and would more accurately describe what we are about. The words 'black' and 'power' together give the impression that we are talking about black domination rather than black equality."[37]

Similar to the sentiments of Wilkins and Young, King was initially concerned with what white people might think of the term "black power." In the summer of 1966 the issue of Black Power became a national debate. Various attempts to illustrate this slogan were made.

According to one observer, there ensued a "New Negro Mood" following the Greenwood incident of 1966:

> Perhaps most Negroes are readier to use force than they used to be: they have less stake than whites in the status quo. . . . The new Negro mood is at once

more militant and more race-conscious. A new Negro readiness to fight will be evident, however, not just in the red-hot fringe but in a more general assertiveness and even arrogance. Whites should be prepared for this.[38]

It was also insisted upon, within the national press, that black power had to be defined.

> The civil rights movement in America has stumbled badly over a phrase that so far has defied every attempt at definition. The words quickly became a part of the vocabulary of protest. But it was left to each user of the phrase to define it as he saw fit. . . . The situation has finally hardened with CORE and SNCC holding to the "black power" formula and all the other major rights organizations condemning it.[39]

The civil rights coalition, from 1966 to 1968, was preoccupied with the semantics and the concept of "black power." Black Americans expressed frustration at not being able to clearly and distinctly define the meaning behind the term. The debate over black power tore the coalition asunder. Gene Roberts, a *New York Times* reporter and an eyewitness to many of the "schisms" endured by the coalition, observed that "There is something intoxicating about the chant black power. It leads Stokely Carmichael to talk of tearing down court houses and it leads Willie Ricks, an aide to Mr. Carmichael, to mutter that "white blood will flow."[40] More importantly, there was something disturbing about the fact that those within in the coalition who supported the term were initially told that they, "shouldn't say black power" because it had threatening overtones—to white people.

The threat of Black Power was recognized by both the defenders and the detractors of the term.

> even within the Negro community itself, "black power" has touched off a major debate—the most bitter the community has experienced since the days of Booker T. Washington and W.E.B. Du Bois, and one which threatens to ravage the entire civil rights movement. Indeed, a serious split has already developed between advocates of black power like Floyd McKissick of CORE and Stokely Carmichael of SNCC, on the one hand, and Dr. Martin Luther King of SCLC, Roy Wilkins of the NAACP, and Whitney Young of the Urban League, on the other.[41]

As Bayard Rustin predicted, the debate over "black power" ravaged the coalition. This was at a time when the coalition had just savored its most significant achievements. There should be no mistaking that this coalition was responsible for the greatest civil rights measures for African Americans since Reconstruction. It could have gone further. But while Martin Luther King, Jr. eventually saw that Black Power, if employed properly, "was a positive and legitimate call to action," Roy Wilkins insisted it meant "going it alone and had racist overtones." While Whitney Young contended that power "is neither black nor white," Stokely Carmichael and James McKissick asserted that blacks should be able to define their own terms.

Although one could add several names to the list of detractors and defenders of Black Power, Stokely Carmichael of SNCC, Floyd McKissick of CORE, and James Forman of SNCC can be identified as the lead articulators of Black Power. Martin Luther King, Jr., within the last few month of his life, provided an eloquent defense of the concept as well. Each individual offered concrete literary justifications in defense of the concept of Black Power from the vanguard, and were its most reasonably ardent defenders.

Black Power became the official platform of SNCC and CORE after 1966. During their 23rd annual convention, under the direction of Floyd McKissick, the CORE adopted a resolution to embrace "Black Power."[42] Former National Director James Farmer resigned from CORE after the Greenwood incident. Stokely Carmichael replaced John Lewis as Chairman of SNCC in May 1966. By the end of that same year, Lewis turned in his resignation with the organization altogether. Also in the Spring of 1966, the SNCC Atlanta Project separatists, lead by SNCC organizer Bill Ware, issued a separatist position paper on the new direction of SNCC.

> Negroes in this country have never been allowed to organize themselves because of white interference. As a result of this, the stereotype has been reinforced that blacks cannot organize themselves. The white psychology that blacks have to be watched, also reinforces this stereotype. Blacks, in fact, feel intimidated by the presence of whites, because of their knowledge of the power that whites have over their lives. . . . If people must express themselves freely, there has to be a climate in which they can do this. . .In an attempt to find a solution to our dilemma, we propose that our organization (S.N.C.C.) should be black-staffed, black-controlled and black-financed.[43]

The "black power" stance not only divided the coalition, but it ripped SNCC apart as Carmichael drifted away from the organization toward Pan-African socialism, and Forman moved toward racial separatism. No one could define "black power." The lack of ideological continuity surrounding the concept of Black Power illustrates the problem of self-identity in the black community. The central theme of Black Power advocates was black self-determinism and black self-identity, but their was no unified response for either. Their existed a plethora of examples for black self-identity. How would black Americans self-identify? The advocates of separation, integration, and pluralism were engaged in a heated discourse over this subject as it related to the 'black power' stance.

While all three rejected the integrationist model to empowerment, and unified in their commitment to independent black organization, there was never a clear common solution to the concept of Black Power to replace the integrationist model. Stokely Carmichael's initial pluralist approach became Pan-African in nature, as he attempted to establish a link with the Black Panther Party. He eventually severed all ties with that Party too. He was expelled from SNCC in 1968, and went on to become a special advisor to Kwame Nkrumah's All African Peoples Revolutionary Party in 1969. He became a close advisor to Guinean President Sekou Ture—hence in his new persona Kwame Ture. While Floyd McKissick repeatedly defined "black power" as the pooling of black political and economic resources, the term got away from Stokely Carmichael for whom the term meant different things at variant instances including political pluralism and cultural nationalism. James Forman seemed to fully embrace the concept of separatism in his "Black Manifesto," delivered in 1969, which called for reparations from the "colonizing forces of the white Christian churches."[44]

McKissick, like Carmichael, argued that blacks must take control over the basic functions of their personal community. But McKissick believed black empowerment could be achieved through the system, by the means of adaptation. According to McKissick, in his essay "Black Power Defined," African Americans could achieve their power if they could "act in the framework of this democracy." Although McKissick's justifications are generally pluralist in nature as he defined Black Power as the "mobilization of the black community as a political, social and economic bloc," their are shades of Garvey's economic entrepreneurship and separatism within his philosophy as well:

> We need many more black-owned businesses in our black communities, employing local residents. Secretarial schools and small business training programs should be supported by government funds. Cooperatives and credit unions should be encouraged.[45]

In his "Black Manifesto" of 1967, McKissick stated that the goal of all black people was self-determinism or the right to "control one's own destiny." McKissick defined this control in such a way, "Black people seek to control the educational system, the political-economic system and the administration of their own communities. They must control their own courts and their own police."[46] McKissick also asserted that this "control" should include the "ownership of land area" in particular places such as Harlem. He insisted that this "land area" could be turned over to the majority of its inhabitants either "individually or collectively."[47] His new community project known as "Soul City" had separatist leanings. McKissick envisioned his future city, located on several acres of farm in Warren County, North Carolina, as a new community supported chiefly by black economic enterprises.[48]

The justifications for Black Power generated by Stokely Carmichael and James Forman led SNCC to embrace racial separatism. The organizations most able leaders, including Carmichael and Forman by 1969, such as Moses, Bond, and Lewis, eventually abandoned the organization altogether. Floyd McKissick resigned from CORE in 1968. He was succeeded by Roy Innis who vowed to make the organization a "separatist" one.

The need for black self-identity forced many Black Power advocates into a defensive stance, and they began to *disassociate* with the group. This was no mere generational divide. James Forman, born in Marshall County, Mississippi in 1928, was nearly forty years old when the vanguard fell apart. At forty-five, Floyd McKissick was one of the oldest yet most important articulators of "black power." Forman was an integral force within SNCC. According to historian Clayborne Carson in his book *In Struggle*, Forman made SNCC what it was and if it were not for his administrative skills the organization would not have achieved as much as it did under his influence. He stayed with the organization for nearly a decade serving in one crucial administrative capacity or another.

James Forman, who briefly became an official of the Black Panther Party as Minister of Education in 1969, after his resignation from SNCC, recognized the lack of ideological continuity regarding "black power," conceding that the slogan was not adequately defined:

> Black Power was not defined adequately at the time. If it had been, the government and its Negroes might not have been able to co-opt the term. Here, we in SNCC must assume some blame, for the term received no precise definition from us. We were stunned and overwhelmed by its immediate success. The most radical definition of Black Power that we could give at the time was "power for black people." Thus the door was left open for opportunists to define the term in any manner they chose. . . . But that is not to excuse our own inability and unwillingness to define the objectives and program for achieving Black Power. We were caught by not having our own revolutionary ideology together.[49]

Forman came to eventually align himself with the separatist approach to black empowerment. James Forman was responsible for opening the modern debate for reparations as compensation for the past suffering of the black community. His 1980 Master's thesis defense at Cornell University contended that because African Americans constituted an "oppressed nation of people," they were therefore entitled to territorial self-determination across the black belt section of the American South.

SNCC and CORE, as organizations, moved well beyond the boundaries of coalition by the end of the decade. Julius Lester, a former SNCC organizer, contended that separation was a "necessity." And in 1967, the Chicago office of SNCC insisted, "We must fill ourselves with hate for all white things."[50] John Churchville, a member of SNCC Atlanta Project, insisted that there had been divisions within the black community since slavery, and these divisions fostered among many blacks a "slave mentality."[51] In his assessment, Churchville insisted that the civil rights movement, as it had advanced until 1966, was a movement to advance the leadership of the white liberals who supported it.

SNCC imploded from within because some in the organization saw disassociation with whites, in the interest of self-identification, as the only way that blacks could achieve and maintain their own power. CORE, a larger, older, and more loosely defined organization of virtually autonomous affiliates, was founded on the principles of interracial coalition. SNCC, a smaller more closely knit "band of brothers and circle of friends," was more vulnerable to collapse, as it eventually did along with the coalition. In 1971, SNCC had no national office. Chairman H. Rap Brown, who took over the post from Carmichael in 1967, was in prison serving a ten year sentence for armed robbery.

Notes

1 Floyd McKissick, "The Civil Rights Movement is Dead," in *The Core Papers-Notes of the Chairman, 1966-1968*, at the King Center.

2 Stokely Carmichael, "Black Power," in *Black Protest: 350 Years of History, Documents, and Analyses*, ed. Joanne Grant, 436 (1968; New York, 1996).

3 This was the assessment of John Lewis regarding the "Black Power" movement.

4 The precursor to CORE was an organization known as FOR (Fellowship of Reconciliation) formed by conscientious objectors during WWI.

5 Although Clayborne Carson in his book *In Struggle* asserts that there were at least 50,000 participants by April of 1960, some estimates are as high as 70,000 or more. In an attempt to utilize this strength the Executive Director of King's SCLC calls for a conference in response.

6 Student Non-Violent Coordinating Committee, "Report of the Raleigh Conference," The SNCC Records1960-1972, The State Historical Society of Wisconsin.

7 The 1946 Supreme Court decision in the *Irene Morgan* case spurned the first "freedom ride" which resulted in prolonged prison terms for some of the participants.

8 Henry Hampton, and Steve Fayer, *Voices of Freedom: An Oral History of the Civil Rights Movement from the 1950s through the 1980s* (New York: Bantam Books: 1991), 94.

9 Ibid.

10 Isabel Wilkerson, "Soul Survivor, From Stokely Carmichael to Kwame Ture." *Essence*, May, 1998, 110.

11 Gloria Styles, Personal interview, July 10, 1998. Gloria Styles insisted that, while the public persona of SNCC was for nonviolence, that the underlying sentiments of SNCC were for retaliation against whites.

12 Adam Fairclough, *Race & Democracy: The Civil Rights Struggle In Louisiana, 1915-1972* (Athens and London: University of Georgia Press, 1995), 342.

13 Henry Hampton and Steve Fayer, *Voices of Freedom: An Oral History of the Civil Rights Movement, from the 1950s Through the 1980s* (New York, 1991) 184.

14 Hampton and Fayer, *Voices of Freedom*, 288. Kwame Ture's reflections upon white participation in the movement.

15 Alvin Poussaint, "How the 'White Problem' Spawned Black Power," *Ebony*, August, 1967, 89.

16 Ibid.

17 Many white volunteers fought alongside SNCC in the battle for the Deep South, including the United States Students Association, the National Association of Students and the Students for a Democratic Society.

18 Student Nonviolent Coordinating Committee, "Position Paper on Black Power," in *Modern Black Nationalism: From Marcus Garvey to Louis Farrakhan*, ed. William L. Van De Burg, (New York: New York University Press, 1997), 120.

19 Steve Max, "Mississippi Freedom Democratic Party: Background and Recent Developments." *The Papers of the Mississippi Freedom Democratic Party-1964, At the King Center for Non violence and Social Justice.*

20 Ibid.

21 Ibid.

22 Cleveland Sellers, *The River of No Return: The Autobiography of a Black Militant and the Life and Death of SNCC* (Jackson and London: University of Mississippi Press, 1973), 108-109.

23 Ibid.

24 Sellers, 130.

25 August Meier and Elliott Rudwick, *CORE: A Study in the Civil Rights Movement 1942-1968* (New York: Oxford University Press, 1973), 329.

26 John Lewis and Michael D'orso, *Walking With the Wind: A Memoir of the Movement* (New York: Simon & Schuster, 1998), 291.

27 Sellers, 137-139.

28 Sellers, 123.

29 Sellers, 151.

30 Sellers, 152.

31 Ibid.

32 Student Nonviolent Coordinating Committee, "Background on the development of political strategy and political education in Lowndes County, Alabama." *The Student Nonviolent Coordinating Committee Records (1959-1972) at the Martin Luther King, Jr. Center for Nonviolent Social Change.*

33 Gene Roberts, "Mississippi Reduces Protection for Marchers," *New York Times*, June 16, 1966, 33.

34 Hamtpon and Fayer, *Voices of Freedom*, 292.

35 Ibid.

36 Congressman Lewis stated in a personal interview that "Stokely showed me a copy of the 1965 commencement address speech of Adam Clayton Powell, Jr. in which Powell repeatedly emphasized the need for Black Power." W.E.B. Du Bois and Richard Wright both, previous to the Carmichael popularization, once mentioned the need for "black power." Of course SNCC was well into demonstrating the use of Black Power in their Atlanta Project program and in Lowndes County.

37 Martin Luther King, Jr., "Where Do We Go from Here: Chaos or Community?" in *Testament of Hope*, 574.

38 "The New Negro Mood," *Life*, June 10, 1966, 4.

39 "Black Power Must be Defined," *Life*, July 22, 1966, 4.

40 Gene Roberts, "Why the Cry for Black Power," *New York Times*, July 3, 1966, 16.

41 Bayard Rustin, "Black Power and Coalition Politics," in *Down the Line: The Collected Writings of Bayard Rustin* by Bayard Rustin, (Chicago,: Quadrangle Books, 1971), 154.

42 "Core Will Insist on 'Black Power,'" *New York Times*, July 5, 1966: 1, 22.

80   *You Can't Say Black Power!*

43 Student Nonviolent Coordinating Committee, "Position Paper on Black Power," in *Modern Black Nationalism: From Marcus Garvey to Louis Farrakhan*, 120-126.

44 James Forman, "From Manifesto to the White Christian Churches and the Jewish Synagogues in the United States of America and All Other Racist Institutions," in *Modern Black Nationalism; From Marcus Garvey to Louis Farrakhan*, ed. William L. Van De Burg, (New York: New York University Press, 1997), 183.

45 Floyd McKissick, "Constructive Militancy," *Papers of the Congress of Racial Equality-Notes of the Chairman-1966, at the King Center for Nonviolent Social Change.*

46 Floyd McKissick, "A Black Manifesto," *The Papers of the Congress of Racial Equality-Notes of the Chairman-1967, at the King Center for Nonviolent Social Change.*

47 Ibid.

48 Although the Soul City Corporation managed to secure a 14 million dollar bond issue guarantee from the Department of Housing and Urban development, the venture fell into difficulty and was eventually taken over by the federal government in 1980.

49 James Forman, *The Making of Black Revolutionaries*, (New York,1972), 459.

50 Student Nonviolent Coordinating Committee, "We Want Black Power," *Black Protest Thought in the Twentieth Century*, ed. August Meier, (Indianapolis and New York: The Bobbs Merrill Company, 1971), 487.

51 John Churchville, "An Analysis of the Civil Rights Movement," *The SNCC Papers-Atlanta Project Papers-1966, at the State Historical Society of Wisconsin.*

Chapter 5

The Panther is a Black Cat

Black is waiting in the darkness;
Black the ground where hoods have lain.
Black is the sorrow—misted story;
Black the brotherhood of pain.
James Emanuel, "Negritude"

The second Black Panther Party adopted the symbol of the panther too as a symbol of black strength. They chose the panther because the panther is a *black* cat. The symbol of the cat was borrowed directly from SNCC. A SNCC volunteer from Oakland, California, who worked in Lowndes County during the summer of 1966, showed the emblem to Huey P. Newton and Bobby Seale upon his return to California—it impressed them.[1] They were experimenters. The experimentalists called themselves many different things. They were revolutionary nationalists, black socialists, Marxists, Marxists-Leninists, among other various labels.

American society was considered to be fundamentally flawed because of white racism for the experimenters. Many experimenters saw the "flaw" of institutionalized racism as inextricably linked to the advance of American capitalism:

> We must remember this country is run by a slave oligarchy and brigandish criminals who have no respect for its people, be they black or white; its primary interest is capitalism. So when we talk about the ideology of the Black Panther Party we are talking about the experiences of Blacks in racist, fascist America.[2]

The experimenters believed that the system would have to be revamped, remodeled, or significantly altered in order to become applicable to American blacks. The experimenters are characterized as such because they were willing to try almost anything, including the threat of violent political overthrow, to remodel a system they saw as inherently corrupt. They shift in and out of alternating categories of the Black Power paradigm. They denounced white America, and yet flirted with the New Left. Some embraced violence, as a means to black liberation, but later renounced it.

The Black Panther Party for Self-Defense, created amid the 1966 Oakland, California riots, comprised a perfect example of the experimental mindset:

> In 1966 we called our Party a Black Nationalist Party. We called ourselves
> Black Nationalists because we thought that nationhood was the answer. Shortly
> after that we decided that what was really needed was revolutionary national-
> ism, that is, nationalism plus socialism. After analyzing conditions a little more,
> we found that it was impractical and even contradictory. Therefore, we went to
> a higher level of consciousness. So we called ourselves Internationalists.. Inter-
> nationalism, if I understand the word, means the interrelationship among a
> group of nations. But since no nation exists, and since the United States is in
> fact an empire, it is impossible for us to be internationalists. These transforma-
> tions and phenomena require us to call ourselves "intercommunalists." . . . The
> Black Panther Party now disclaims internationalism and supports intercom-
> munalism.[3]

Huey P. Newton, as the Black Panther Party's lead theoretician, guided the ideology of the Party into a series of radical transformations from Black Nationalism, through revolutionary nationalism, to intercommunalism. Newton, along
with other influential figures in the organization, failed to direct the Party into a
unified concept of "black" beyond the symbolism of the barrel of the gun, the
provocative black beret, and the color of the cat. Their ideology of black liberation, at the outset, was mostly an aggressive expression.

The Black Panther Party has been described by some as nothing more than a
street gang. Black Panthers were accused, and some convicted, of virtually everything from murder, armed robbery, rape, drug trafficking and substance abuse.
But the Panthers also implemented a variety of noteworthy programs such as a
Free Breakfast program in Berkeley, California, a Free Shoe Program in Richmond, California, a Free Health Clinic in Roxbury, Massachusetts, and a Free
Clothing for Children rally in Harlem, among other significant endeavors.

Although there remains to be a significant amount of controversy surrounding the meaning of the Black Panthers in American history, the specific purpose
of this concluding chapter is to illustrate the Black Panthers as experimenters
and to examine why the Student Nonviolent Coordinating Committee and the
Black Panther Party did not merge. Because the Black Panthers were only indi-
rectly involved with the coalition, the focus will be on the failure of this alliance
between 1966 and 1968. This chapter does not intend to provide a comprehensive critique, nor history, of the Black Panther Party, but *is* an attempt to understand why the Black Panthers failed to produce a new vanguard of unity with
SNCC in the interest of black liberation.

The experimenters were more enamored with the prospect of a change for
the better than they were with conceiving a rigid doctrine of ideas. Individuals
and groups like Malcolm X, through his Organization of African Unity, along
with Robert F. Williams of the Republic of New Africa, and the Black Panther
Party, can all be considered experimenters. None of these groups or individuals
were content with the existing order, and all sought some kind of fundamental
change or alteration to the system. Malcolm's protest ethic included political
pluralism, cultural nationalism, and some have suggested elements of socialism.

He contended that "The Organization of Afro-American Unity would organize the Afro-American community block by block," and at the same time insisted that, "we must launch a cultural revolution to unbrainwash an entire people."[4] Timothy B. Tyson outlined the experimental mindset of Robert F. Williams:

> His militant message was neither racially separatist nor rigidly ideological. Williams stressed black economic advancement, black pride, black culture, independent black political action, and what he referred to as "armed self-reliance." He connected the southern freedom struggle with the anticolonialism of emerging Third World nations, especially in Africa. His approach was practical, eclectic, and improvisational.[5]

The terms "eclectic and improvisational" are good adjectives to describe the experimental mindset. Similar to the ideology of Malcolm X and Robert Williams, the ideology of the Black Panthers was defined. They "experimented" with Black Nationalism, socialism, and communalism.

The Black Panthers employed a myriad of ideas and outlined a number of strategies in their quest for liberation. Committed to social reform through inflammatory rhetoric, propaganda, paramilitary street patrols, and constructive community action, they utilized the African American community as their primary base. More than one Panther, including Bobby Seale, David Hilliard, and Huey P. Newton, described the Black Panther Party as committed to socialist reform or revolution among many other things. But the Party eventually abandoned Black Nationalism, along with their fragile prospects for a merger with the Student Nonviolent Coordinating Committee.

The lack of ideological continuity in the Black Revolution was more evident, and the disputes amongst black revolutionaries were more turbulent. Ideological disagreements between the Black Panthers and Ron Karenga's Us organization became particularly dangerous as related by Elaine Brown:

> The escalating conflict with the Us organization was not so clear. There were frequent incidents, the most treacherous of which involved Panthers selling newspapers on the street. Seven or eight Us members might spring out of a van and pounce upon a Brother or Sister and fire a few rounds. Ronald Freeman had been shot like that. We would retaliate by shooting up their facilities or homes. Those confrontations were actually generating more terror than the conflicts with the pigs.[6]

There existed a dangerous animosity between the cultural nationalists and the Black Panther Party. Ron Karenga, then a social service worker with Los Angeles County, was convinced that his Us organization, a black separatist group formed as a result of the Watts riots in 1965, was the vanguard organization responsible for leading the black masses to revolution through the "introduction of an alternative value system."[7] According to Karenga, black culture, with an emphasis in African tradition, was the vehicle by which liberation would be achieved. Huey P. Newton of the Black Panther Party reserved his most stark criticism for the cultural nationalists, "The cultural nationalist seeks refuge by retreating to some ancient African behavior and culture;" Newton distanced the ideology of the Black Panthers from cultural nationalism, "We do not believe that it is necessary to go back to the culture of 11th century Africa. In reality, we must deal with the dynamic present in order to forge a progressive change."[8] Ideological conflict eventually escalated into violence in the streets. Two Black Panthers, Bunchy Carter and John Huggins, were killed in a 1969 shoot-out with Karenga's group on the campus of UCLA.

The struggle for black equality has materialized through a series of "interrelated and overlapping stages of development," including the fight for freedom from slavery, the quest for civil rights, the journey to socio-economic parity, and the struggle for ethnic identity.[9] The conflict behind this failure to ally occurred because these two organizations, the SNCC and the Black Panthers, met at the crossroads of two interrelated and overlapping stages in the struggle for black equality. The ideological features of the *Black Power Paradigm* shifted, moved, overlapped, and sometimes collided. The quest for black liberation, as Solomon P. Gethers has noted, is comprised of a series of "interrelated stages." The "stage" of civil rights reform, characterized by the goals of public accommodation and voting rights, shifted into the struggle for black identity and the search for socio-economic parity. With the collapse of the coalition for national civil rights reform, the struggle for black equality shifted focus. The stages of ethnic identity and socio-economic reform supplanted issues of civil reform, and subsequently splintered the consensus of coalition within the struggle for black equality. This level of ideological fragmentation and discontinuity in black protest thought only became more pronounced in the black liberation movement after 1966.

The struggle for black equality, marshaled under the emblem of the black cat, which had rapidly become a symbol of black unity and militancy, had become significantly unclear. James Forman of SNCC, who in his memoirs considered that "black power was not adequately defined at the time," recognized at least three groups in California alone who made an attempt to organize around "the symbol of the black panther."[10] These groups, as identified by Forman, included the Black Panther Party for Self-Defense, the Black Panther Party of Northern California, and the Black Panther Party of Southern California. Forman also contends that, as SNCC moved toward forging an alliance with the Panthers, there were also other organizations in the Los Angeles area, such as Ron Karenga's Us and the Black Congress, "hassling" for liberation.[11] It was a time of confusion and disorganization. The *Black Power Paradigm* became like a mixture of alphabet soup by the end of the decade, including such organizations as SNCC, CORE, Us, the BPP, the RNA, the BLA, and RAM along with a series of other local and community organizations such as NEGRO.

The fight for black equality *has* to be understood as a dynamic struggle that has managed to unearth a *multi-tiered* level of oppression which has subsequently generated a series of parallel concerns and objectives. This has added to the level of confusion: Where should liberation begin, and where does it *end*? Civil rights reform, ethnic identity, and socio-economic equality were all valid concerns. In the Black Power battle of the 1960s, the distinctions between *means* and *end* became blurred, while the overall goals, and there were many, became completely overwhelming. *Where does liberation begin, and where does it end?* This question has beleaguered the evolution of black protest thought since emancipation, and only became more pronounced in the 1960s. The movement for national civil rights reform was not expansive enough, as it existed before 1966, to contain the multiplicity of concerns regarding African American progress.

Although a number of contributing factors can be attributed to the failed alliance between SNCC and the BPP, such as the unmitigated level of repression from the FBI, the clash of organizational structures, as well as personality conflicts, the concern here will be upon the shift in ideological focus. SNCC, with their experience in the Deep South, placed a greater emphasis with the struggle for black identity and their belief in power for black people—under black leadership. The Panthers concentrated on issues of class struggle, and eventually dismissed Black Nationalism. The Black Panthers, with their embrace of a socialist critique of the black experience, increased ties with the white Left after 1966.

"The creation of the Party by Huey P. Newton and Bobby Seale was the extension of work that many of us in the SNCC had been doing over the past seven years and a natural outgrowth of the intense struggle that had been waged since 1960," stated James Forman.[12] Because of the "political need" to increase the chances of survival, for the SNCC and the black liberation struggle in general, some in the SNCC actively accepted overtures from the Black Panthers for support and collaboration, "It was in this spirit that Stokely Carmichael, George Ware, and Rap Brown of SNCC talked with the group on various occasions in 1966 and early 1967."[13] In 1967, Bobby Seale and Eldridge Cleaver "drafted" several leading SNCC members into the Party. Cleaver, the group's Minister of Information, himself was introduced to the Party in February of 1967. After an altercation with police in October of 1967, Huey P. Newton was arrested, on charges of manslaughter. The two groups would rally around the banner of "Free Huey" and attempt to forge a new alliance.

It was Eldridge Cleaver, a former convict and writer for the New Left journal *Ramparts*, who guided the Party toward the white Left. Through the mechanizations of Cleaver, the Black Panthers forged alliances outside of the parameters of the black liberation movement; the Peace and Freedom Party eventually ran Cleaver for President of the United States. The Black Panthers were able to form ties with such organizations as the Young Lords, a segment of the Puerto Rican political movement, the Brown Berets, a group of Mexican American activists, the Young Patriots comprised of lower income whites, and the American contingent of Mao Tse Tung's Red Guards. By the end of the decade, "black power" had become understood as "people's power" according to the Black Panthers lead theoretician.[14]

The alliance between SNCC and the Black Panthers was eventually de-

stroyed by the Panther's intimate ties with the white Left. Elaine Brown spoke
of these "intimate ties" in her book *A Taste of Power:*

> Whatever the hazards of association, the Black Panther Party seemed to make a
> place in the sun for sympathetic whites. White artists were the first to come in
> out of the cold. As Los Angeles and New York were the main homes of the ar-
> tistic communities of America fostered, the party chapters there began develop-
> ing relationships with liberal and progressive white artists. In New York, there
> were such notable supporters as Leonard Bernstein. Our chapter in Southern
> California, however, was becoming the beneficiary of the support of the most
> powerful collection of artists in America: the Hollywood film industry's actors,
> actresses, producers, writers and directors.[15]

While Newton, Seale, and Cleaver became enamored by the idea of a socialist
revolution, through political alliances with the white Left, Stokely Carmichael
and James Forman stressed the need for black power for black people, under the
tutelage of black leadership.

James Forman gave an incendiary speech in Berkley, California on February 4, 1968 in which he declared that black people were not prepared to "abdi-
cate our leadership to anybody," as he went on to state, "We are not going to
share the leadership, and that should be crystal clear. We are not going to give
up the leadership and then have our struggle aborted as we have seen it aborted
in the labor struggle movement in this country, as we have seen it aborted many
other times."[16] According to Forman, this speech served as a warning to "many
who would call themselves white radicals or revolutionaries."[17] Some in SNCC,
especially after their defeat at the 1964 Democratic National Convention, believed that their movement had been "aborted," or co-opted by white liberals
and with it the role of black leadership in the cause. They were not prepared to
let this happen again. The rhetoric of James Forman and Stokely Carmichael
drifted away from political pluralism into black separatism after 1966.

"Politically, decisions which affect black lives have always been made by
white people—the "white power structure."[18] The white Left were contained
within this power structure, according to Carmichael. In order for black liberation to occur, black people had to first develop a sense of self and a sense of
community. A strong alliance had to exist within the black community first, and
this was the motivation behind SNCC's collaborative overtures to the Black
Panthers, before valid coalitions could be sought outside of the black community. "Black people must first ask themselves what is good for them, and then
they can determine if the "liberal" is willing to coalesce. They must recognize
that institutions and political organizations have no consciences outside of their
own special interests," was Carmichael's view on alliances outside of the black
community.[19] His travels in Africa, through 1968, convinced him that Pan-Africanism was the most legitimate expression of "black power." He abandoned political pluralism for black separatism, as he was virtually ousted from the SNCC
in 1968, and literally purged from the Black Panthers in 1969. James Forman
resigned his position with the Panthers in 1969 as well. Eldridge

Cleaver accused Stokely Carmichael of being blind—blinded by the color of the cat. Cleaver held Carmichael's emphasis on a Black United Front, in the interest of black liberation, in scathing disdain:

> Within the ranks of your Black United Front you wanted to include the Cultural Nationalists, the Black Capitalist, and the Professional Uncle Toms. You had great dreams in those days, Stokely, and your visions, on the top side, were heroic. On the bottom side, when it came to the details of reality, your vision was blind. You were unable to distinguish your friends from your enemies because all you could see was the color of the cat's skin. It was this blindness that led you to the defense of Adam Clayton Powell, that jackal from Harlem, when he came under attack by his brother jackals in Congress. In short, your habit of looking at the world through black-colored glasses would lead you, on the domestic level, to close ranks with such enemies of black people as James Farmer, Whitney Young, Roy Wilkins and Ron Karenga.[20]

Cleaver thought the idea of Carmichael's embrace of Pan-African sentiments ridiculous, "I think that you should know that the brothers in Africa who are involved in armed struggle against the colonialists would like nothing better than for you to pack up your suit case full of African souvenirs and split back to babylon."[21] The sentiments of Eldridge Cleaver were echoed by Huey Newton:

> the black Panther Party does not subscribe to "Black Power" as such. Not the "Black Power" that has been defined by Stokely Carmichael and Nixon. They seem to agree upon the stipulated definition of "Black Power" which is no more than Black capitalism. That definition is reactionary and certainly not a philosophy that would meet the interest of the people. It would only support the interest of a small group of people. Stokely Carmichael has further stated that Pan-Africanism is the highest expression of "Black Power." We say that Pan-Africanism is the highest expression of cultural nationalism. The Black Panther Party is internationalist.[22]

Newton also "took issue" with Carmichael's emphasis on white racism as the root of the problem by asserting that, "the roots of the racism is based upon the profit motive and capitalism."[23] But it would seem as if Huey P. Newton was blinded, or at least overly concerned, with the color of the cat as well when he admonished William Patterson of the Communist Party, U.S.A. who claimed, "It is apparent to any sane person that Blacks are the vanguard of the struggle against imperialism in the U.S."[24] Huey P. Newton and Stokely Carmichael were correct in asserting that the issues of race and class were paramount in the struggle for black equality.

The atmosphere of paranoia, mistrust, and confusion increased as the Black Panthers fell victim to the same internal strife that plagued SNCC. It was a time of disorganized thinking about the color of the *black* cat. It was a time when several remedies were experimented with in order to solve the problem of racial oppression that had multiple symptoms. The introduction of massive repression from law enforcement agencies nationwide compounded the confusion. The psychological implications were certainly heightened by this repression, as the Black Panthers began to look at one another with suspicious fright. Black radicals shot at the cops, as well as each other. The pressures of this multi-tiered oppression were guided by the self-hatred fostered by the degradation of black people in American society. Suspicions became escalated, and at times were actually generated by the FBI.[25] Eldridge Cleaver understood how this self-hatred influenced the nature of black protest thought:

> in American Negroes, this ethnic self-hatred often takes the bizarre form of a racial death-wish, with many and elusive manifestations. Ironically, it provides much of the impetus behind the motivations of integration. And the attempt to suppress or deny such drives in one's psyche leads many American Negroes to become ostentatious separationists, Black Muslims, and back-to-Africa advocates.[26]

Huey Newton and Bobby Seale made a hasty attempt, by the end of the decade, to reshape the paramilitary image of the Black Panther Party, as they abandoned Black Nationalism and embraced the white Left. While many in SNCC came to embrace racial separatism, others denounced the Black Panthers for "changing the complexion of the meeting" by inviting whites into the alliance of black revolutionaries. By the end of the decade, many black revolutionaries were either in jail, in exile, or deceased. As Huey P. Newton and Bobby Seale eventually came to realize, they never had a chance.

Notes

1 Charlie Cobb, "Revolution: From Stokely Carmichael To Kwame Ture," *Black Scholar* 27 (Fall/Winter, 1997): 37.

2 David Hilliard, "What You Speak So Loud, I Hardly Hear What You Say," *The Black Panther*, November 8, 1969, 9-10.

3 Huey P. Newton, "Speech Delivered at Boston College," in *To Die For the People: The Writings of Huey P. Newton*, ed. Toni Morrison, (1971; New York: Writers and Readers Publishers, 1995), 31-32.

4 Malcolm X, "Malcolm X Founds the Organization of Afro-American Unity," in *Black Protest Though In the Twentieth Century*, ed. August Meier, 413-421 (Indianapolis and New York, 1971).

5 Timothy B. Tyson, "Black Power and the Roots of the African American Freedom Struggle," *Journal of American History* 85 (September 1998): 559.

6 Elaine Brown, *A Taste of Power: A Black Woman's Story* (New York: Anchor Books-Doubleday, 1992), 184.

7 Scot Ngozi-Brown, "The US Organization , Maulana Karenga, and Conflict with the Black Panther Party," *Journal of Black Studies* 28, (November 1997): 157.

8 Huey P. Newton, "The Black Panthers," *The Black Panther*, August 23, 1969, 9-10.

9 Solomon P. Gethers, "Black Nationalism and Human Liberation," *Black Scholar* (May 1970): 45.

10 James Forman, *The Making of Black Revolutionaries* (New York: The Macmillan Company, 1972), 523.

11 Ibid.

12 Forman, *Black Revolutionaries*, 527.

13 Forman, 523.

14 Huey P. Newton, "Huey Newton Talks to the Movement About the Black Panther Party, Cultural Nationalism, SNCC, Liberals and White Revolutionaries," in *The Black Panthers Speak*, ed. Philip S. Foner, (1970; New York: Da Capo Press, 1995), 66.

15 Elaine Brown, *A Taste of Power: A Black Woman's Story* (New York: Anchor Books-Doubleday, 1992), 209.

16 Forman, *Black Revolutionaries*, 525.

17 Ibid.

18 Stokely Carmichael and Charles V. Hamilton, *Black Power: the Politics of Liberation* (New York: Random House, 1967), 7.

19 Carmichael and Hamilton, *Black Power*, 78-79.

20 Eldridge Cleaver, "Open Letter to Stokely Carmichael," *The Black Panther*, August 16, 1969, 5.

21 Ibid.

22 Huey P. Newton, "On the Middle East," in *To Die For the People,* ed. Toni Morrison, (1972; New York: Writers and Readers Publishers, 1995), 192.

23 Ibid.

24 Huey P. Newton, "Reply to William Patterson," in Toni Morrison, ed. *To Die For the People* (1972; New York: Writers and Readers Publishers, 1995), 173.

25 Bobby Seale, along with several other Panthers, was charged with the murder of Alex Rackley, a suspected FBI informant and Panther member, in March 1969.

26 Eldridge Cleaver, *Soul On Ice* (1968; New York: Laurel, 1991), 99.

Chapter 6

The Dream Deferred

What happens to a dream deferred?
Langston Hughes, "Harlem"

"This is a new day, we don't sing those words any more. In fact, the whole song should be discarded. Not 'We Shall Overcome,' but 'We Shall Overrun,' stated one disgruntled civil rights worker to Martin Luther King, Jr. during the James Meredith March Against Fear in 1966.[1] Survived is a better word than overcome. The relationship between black people and America has been an abusive one. The history of oppression has produced high levels of antagonism, anger, self-hatred, self-abuse and depression within the black community. Psychologists have come to conclude that abuse takes a toll on the body and the mind. When a body is abused it often reaches a level of great exhaustion or death. Of course, one could make the argument that King's dream of the Beloved Community was merely a utopian vision. Integration was never completely defined beyond suggestions of assimilation and remains an "ethical dilemma." America is not an integrated society. Some are simply more integrated than others.

The struggle for black equality in America has been a comprehensive struggle for economic, social, and legal recognition. African Americans have gained and progressed since the Civil Rights Movement on many different levels but the physical and mental health of black America is not good. A disproportionate number of African Americans suffer from high blood pressure, diabetes, depression and HIV-AIDS. African American males constitute a staggering 40% of the nation's prison population while the U.S. Department of Justice indicates that African American males are more than 80% likely to end up under penal supervision over the course of a lifetime as opposed to the 17% for white males. Roughly 50% of African Americans drop out of school without earning a high school diploma. More than 80% of the new HIV-AIDS cases are African American women. According to national statistics, 70% of students on historically black college campuses are African American women. The homicide rate for African American males per 100,000 is soaring and at one point was as high as 72% in the late 1990s. The recognition of African Americans as human beings worthy of equal opportunity and socio-economic parity remains a major problem in the United States today. Hurricane Katrina and its aftermath recently

reinforced how racist America remains today. African Americans died on national television before the eyes of the world. Exhausted, thirsty, and hungry
African Americans died in the streets of New Orleans in 2005.

African Americans did not overcome as a result of the Civil Rights Movement nor did they overrun. While we should recognize that legal segregation
was destroyed by the activism of the organizations involved in the movement,
and with it, the improved socio-economic status of African Americans has occurred, full human dignity has yet to be gained. This is a matter of perception.
The perception of African Americans, as somehow less than human, works to
facilitate low self-esteem among African Americans which ultimately leads to
self-destructive behaviors. African Americans have fought valiantly and consistently against the distortion of the black image in the white mind through sub-
version but the abuse of the black self has also been coupled with poverty, unemployment and generally a concerted institutionalized effort to suppress black
equality.

The breakdown of vanguard unity was most unfortunate. Some serious
questions about black identity were super-imposed over the obstacles of strategy
and methodology in black protest thought that made the Civil Rights *movement*
into the impossible revolution. What happened to the revolution? Integration
seems possible, territorial separatism the most impractical, experimentalism too
unclear, and pluralism the most plausible. What happened to the revolution? The
cultural nationalists won! The Black Power Movement was largely a cultural
and intellectual revolution. Those who argued for the preservation of a distinc-
tive and separate cultural identity for African Americans are now a part of the
Academy. Ron Karenga sold his image to the United States postal service.
Kwanzaa has appeared on an American stamp! The new black consciousness
ushered in by Stokely Carmichael's "Black Power!" has survived within African
American Studies, Black Studies, and Africana Studies programs around the
country.

As the Civil Rights Movement expanded geographically, issues of gender,
class, and sexuality became more pronounced within the coalition and the nation. The Gender studies assessment of the movement contends that women
working from within coalition ranks orchestrated a "second wave" of women's
rights activism. Traditional studies of the Civil Rights Movement often place
middle class African Americans at the forefront of the cause while more recent
scholarship suggests that the movement was indeed a movement of the black
working class both north and south. Queer Studies theorists postulate that the
Stone Wall riots were produced by the ferment of civil rights activism that en-
gulfed the country. The sixties scholar Terry Anderson has written of the 1960s
as "a movement." Although the primary focus of this study has been the breakdown of coalition and the question of black identity, it is pertinent to note that as
the movement expanded the variables of gender, class, and sexuality only compounded issues of strategy and methodology in black protest thought. The question of black identity is multifaceted and includes considerations of gender,
class, and sexuality. Any assessment of the overall movement must consider

these variables.

African American women have always played an integral role in the institutional development of the African American freedom struggle from abolitionism to the present. Many have indeed argued that African American women were at the forefront of civil rights activism before the Civil Rights Movement became a mass movement in the 1950s. The activism of these women has been well documented. African American women created institutions, alliances, and ideologies for the advance of black rights before the 1960s. Mary Church Terrell and Ida B. Wells through the National Association of Colored Women (NACW) established in 1895 supported social service programs for African Americans and spoke out against lynching. Both women played an important role in the creation of the NAACP in 1909. The National Council of Negro Women (NCNW) propelled education advocate Mary McCloud Bethune to the national stage through the 1930s. Irene Morgan refused to give up her seat on a bus in 1947 before Rosa Parks sat down in 1955. Through their activism black women such as SCLC's Ella Baker, NAACP lawyers Constance Baker Motely and Marion Wright Edelman, as well as Ruby Doris Smith and Donna Richards of SNCC further shaped the movement significantly. The activism of these women produced a reaction with the development of black feminism in reaction to the hegemonic masculinities that burst forth from the coalition with such personalities as Eldridge Cleaver.

The African American middle class has expanded significantly since 1960 but so has the black underclass. Through the 1990s, African Americans were three times more represented on the nation's poverty rolls as compared to whites. Many of the activists and leaders in the key organizations were representative of the already emergent black middle class before the 1960s. In the 1990s, an estimated 1 in 4 African Americans were considered middle class. This is significant growth from the 2% in 1960. Class along with gender can both be considered important variables in the decline of civil rights activism after the 1960s. Many of the stated goals outlined by the civil rights leadership have indeed been *legally* secured including such measures as equal access to public facilities and voting rights yet how does one reconcile the social statistics of black American which indicate both gain and loss?

This work has also been a call for a more interdisciplinary approach to the study of the history of African Americans. It is impossible to study the history of African Americans without recognizing the impact of the psychological assault on the African American mind and body in American history. We must begin to look at the relationship between African Americans and the United States of America as one that involves abuse, tragedy and sometimes tremendous triumph.

Notes

1 Martin Luther King, Jr., "Where Do We Go From Here: Chaos or Community?" in *A Testament of Hope: The Essential Writings of Martin Luther King, Jr.*, ed. James Washington, (New York: Harper Collins, 1986), 570.

Glossary

Afro-centrism

A political, cultural, and scholarly movement that promotes an African centered worldview of history.

Affirmative Action

Series of measures instituted to ensure equal opportunity to employment, housing, and education for groups such as ethnic minorities and women previously discriminated against in the past.

Albany Movement

A grouped formed in Albany, Georgia November, 1961 among local activists and members of SNCC. This movement failed to accomplish immediate goals to desegregate the city.

Black Nationalism

Phrase associated with the collection of African American movements emphasizing black racial pride, self-determinism, self-help, and black political autonomy.

Black Power

Slogan popularized by Stokely Carmichael in Mississippi 1966 during the James Meredith March Against Fear emphasizing black self-help and self-determinism.

Bloody Sunday

March 7, 1965 vicious attack on civil rights workers on a 54 mile trek from Selma to Montgomery across the Edmund Pettus Bridge. This incident led to the signing of the Voting Rights Act of 1965.

Boynton v. Virginia

Supreme Court decision in 1960 which held that racial segregation in public transportation terminals was illegal.

Brow V. Board

Brown v. the Board of Education of Topeka, Kansas was the landmark Supreme Court renunciation of the doctrine of "separate but equal" in the public school system delivered in 1954.

Civil Rights Act-1964

Legislation that guaranteed equal access to public facilities; barred discrimination in the workplace on the basis of gender, race and class; creation of the Equal Employment Opportunity Commission.

Civil Rights Act-1965   Legislation that led to the end of obstacles to the ballot such as the poll tax and literacy tests.

EEOC   Agency created in 1964 to oversee the prevention of discrimination in the workplace and later received the power to initiate litigation in this process.

Freedom Rides   Demonstrations led by CORE in 1961 to test compliance in the desegregation of interstate transportation facilities.

Freedom Summer   A large-scale voter-registration project in the Deep South instigated by Bob Moses of SNCC in 1964 involving hundreds of white students from northern Universities.

FOR   Fellowship of Reconciliation an International Christian pacifist organization formed in 1914 to protest World War I and supported racial integration.

Jim Crow   Caricature based on negative black stereotypes that became associated with the laws of segregation.

Kwanzaa   African American secular holiday celebration created by Maulana Karenga inspired by African customs.

Kerner Commission   Commission established by President Lyndon Johnson in 1967 under the direction of Otto Kerner to investigate the causes of civil unrest. The commission found that economic deprivation and racial discrimination played a significant role in the causes of the riots in the 1960s.

LDEF   The Legal Defense and Education Fund was the legal arm of the NAACP that continuously brought suit against segregation statutes.

March Against Fear   Civil rights activist James Meredith's attempt in the summer of 1966 to walk through the state of Mississippi "without fear."

March on Washington   The largest civil rights demonstration "for jobs and freedom" on August 28, 1963

MIA   Montgomery Improvement Association was the precursor to the SCLC created during the Montgomery Bus Boycott.

Morgan v. Virginia   Supreme court decision in 1946 that invalidated segregation on interstate carriers as a result of the activism of Irene Morgan.

New Left   The collection of student activists in the 1960s radicalized by the civil rights movement and who advocated for sweeping progressive changes to American society.

**Non-violent
Direct Action**   Strategy employed by SCLC, CORE, and SNCC to secure equal rights through boycotts, sit-ins, and demonstrations.

Plessy V. Ferguson   Supreme Court decision of 1896 designating "separate but equal" facilities as legal.

Sit-ins   Direct action tactic employed by college students by "sitting in" at lunch counters across the Deep South.

Southern Manifesto   Document written in 1956 supported by 96 southern congressman opposed to racial integration.

Watts Riots   Race riot in south Los Angeles August 11, 1965 precipitated by a series of issues such as poverty, unemployment, and police brutality.

Bibliography

Archives

The Records of the Congress of Racial Equality 1944-1972, at the Martin Luther King, Jr. Center for Nonviolent Social Change, 449 Auburn Avenue N.E., Atlanta, Georgia

The CORE Papers, at the State Historical Society of Wisconsin, 816 State Street, Madison, Wisconsin

The Papers of the Mississippi Freedom Democrats, at the Martin Luther King, Jr. Center for Nonviolent Social Change, 449 Auburn Avenue N.E., Atlanta, Georgia

The Records of the NAACP, Part III and Part IV, in the Manuscript Division, at the Library of Congress, 101 Independence Avenue, S. E., Washington, D. C.

The Records of the National Urban League, Part II and Part III, in the Manuscript Division, at the Library of Congress, 101 Independence Avenue, S. E., Washington, D.C.

The Papers of Roy Wilkins (1901-1980), in the Manuscript Division, at the Library of Congress, 101 Independence Avenue, S. E., Washington, D. C.

The SNCC Papers-Atlanta Project Papers 1960-1972, at the State Historical Society of Wisconsin, 816 State Street, Madison, Wisconsin

The Southern Christian Leadership Conference Papers 1954-1970, at the Martin Luther King, Jr. Center for Nonviolent Social Change, 449 Auburn Avenue N.E., Atlanta, Georgia

The Student Nonviolent Coordinating Committee Records 1959-1972, Martin Luther King, Jr. Center for Nonviolent Social Change, 449 Auburn Avenue N.E., Atlanta, Georgia

Books

Adeleke, Tunde. *Un-African Americans: Nineteenth –Century Black Nationalists and the Civilizing Mission.* Lexington: University of Kentucky Press, 1998.

Allen, Ernest, Jr. "Religious Heterodoxy and Nationalist Tradition: The Continuing Evolution of the Nation of Islam." *The Black Scholar* 26 (Fall-Winter 1996): 2-35.

Baldwin, James. *Notes of A Native Son.* 1955; Boston: Beacon Press, 1984.

Baldwin, James. *The Fire Next Time.* New York: The Dial Press, 1963.

Baldwin, James. "A Talk With Teachers." *Saturday Review* December 21, 1963,174-179.

Black Panther Party. "The Black Panther Party Stands for Revolutionary Solidarity." In *The Black Panthers Speak,* edited by Philip S. Foner, 220-223. New York: DA Capo Press, 1995.

Brown, Elaine. *A Taste of Power: A Black Woman's Story.* New York: Anchor Books-

Doubleday, 1992.

Brown, H. Rap. *Die, Nigger, Die!* New York: Dial Press, 1969.

Baraka, Amiri. "Malcolm As Ideology." In *Malcolm In Our Own Image*, edited by Joe Wood, 90-98. New York: St. Martins Press, 1992.

Bell, Derrick. *Faces At The Bottom of The Well: The Permanence of Racism*. New York: Basic Books - Harper Collins, 1992.

Bennett, Lerone, Jr. *Before the Mayflower: A History of Black America*. 5th ed. New York: Penguin Books, 1988.

Blank, Jonah. "The Muslim Mainstream: Islam is Growing Fast in America, And its Members Defy Stereotypes." *U.S. News & World Report* July 20, 1998, 22 - 26.

Bogle, Donald. *Toms, Coons, Mulattos, Mammies, and Bucks: An Interpretive History of Blacks in American Films*. New York: Continuum, 1994.

Carmichael, Stokely. "Comments by Stokely Carmichael, Chairman of the Student Non-Violent Coordinating Committee." *Notes of the Chairman-1966*, The Student Non-Violent Coordinating Committee Records (1959-1972) at the King Center.

Carmichael, Stokely, and Charles V. Hamilton. *Black Power: the Politics of Liberation in America*. New York: Random House, 1967.

Carmichael, Stokely. "What We Want." In *Chronicles Of Negro Protest: A Background Book Documenting the History of Black Power*, edited by Bradford Chambers, New York: Parents' Magazine, 1968.

Carmichael, Stokely. "Black Power." In *Black Protest: 350 Years of History, Documents, and Analyses*, edited by Joanne Grant, 435-441.1968; New York: Fawcett Columbine, 1996.

Carson, Clayborne. *In Struggle: SNCC and the Black Awakening of the 1960s*. Cambridge: Harvard University Press, 1981.

Cobb, Charlie. "Revolution: From Stokely Carmichael to Kwame Ture." *The Black Scholar* 27 (Fall/Winter 1997): 32 - 40.

Cleaver, Eldridge. *Soul On Ice*. 1968; New York: Laurel, 1992.

Cleaver, Eldridge. "Open Letter to Stokely Carmichael." *The Black Panther*, August 16, 1969, 5.

Cleaver, Eldridge. "On Meeting the Needs of the People." *The Black Panther*, August 16, 1969: 4.

Cohen, Jerry, and William S. Murphy. "Burn Baby Burn." *Life*, July 15, 1966, 30-38.

Cruse, Harold. *The Crisis of the Negro Intellectual*. New York: William Morrow & Company Inc., 1967.

Delany, Martin Robison. *The Condition, Elevation, Emigration, And Destiny of Colored People of the United States*. 1852; New York: Arno Press and The New York Times: 1968.

Dittmer, John. *Local People: The Struggle for Civil Rights in Mississippi*. Urbana and Chicago: University of Illinois Press, 1994.

Du Bois, W.E. B. *The Souls of Black Folks*. 1903; New York: Signet Classics, 1982.

Echols, Alice. *Daring to be Bad: Radical Feminism in America 1967-1975*. Minneapolis: University of Minnesota Press, 1989.

Ellison, Ralph. *Invisible Man*. 1947; New York: Vintage International, 1990.

Fairclough, Adam. *Race and Democracy: The Civil Rights Struggle in Louisiana, 1915 – 1972*. Athens and London: The University of Georgia Press, 1995.

Fairclough, Adam. *To Redeem the Soul of America: The Southern Christian Leadership Conference and Martin Luther King, Jr.*. Athens: University of Georgia Press, 1987.

Farmer, James; and Malcolm X. "Separatism V. Integration." In *Black Protest Thought in the Twentieth Century*, edited by August Meier, 2nd ed. Indianapolis and New York:The Bobbs Merrill Company, Inc., 1971.

Fanon, Frantz. "Concerning Violence." In *Modern Black Nationalism from Marcus Garvey to Louis Farrakhan*, edited by William L. Van De Burg, 128-132. New York: New York University Press, 1997.

Finkelman, Paul. *Dred Scott V. Sanford_*. Boston: Bedford Books, 1997.

Forman, James. *The Making of Black Revolutionaries*. New York: The Macmillan Company, 1972.

Forman, James. "Black Manifesto." *Modern Black Nationalism from Marcus Garvey to Louis Farrakhan*, edited by William L. Van De Burg, 180-183. New York: New York University Press, 1997.

Forman, James. "From Which Way the Black Belt Thesis." In *Modern Black Nationalism from Marcus Garvey to Louis Farrakhan*, edited by William L. Van De Burg, 183-187. New York: New York University Press, 1997.

Fraser, Gerald. "SNCC Breaks Ties With Stokely Carmichael." *New York Times*, August 23, 1968, 16.

Gaddis, Frederick. Personal Interview. 30 Nov. 1998.

Gannon, Bill. "Races Split of Rating Troopers." *Sunday Star Ledger*, May 17, 1998, 1, 16.

Garnet, Henry Highland. "Henry Highland Garnet Calls On the Slaves to Resist." In John L. Thomas, ed. *Slavery Attacked: The Abolitionist Crusade*. Englewood Cliffs: Prentice hall, 1965.

Garvey, Marcus. "Declaration of Rights of the Negro Peoples of the World." In *Modern Black Nationalism from Marcus Garvey to Louis Farrakhan*, edited by William L. Van De Burg, 150-152. New York: New York University Press, 1997.

Gethers, Solomon P. "Black Nationalism And Human Liberation." *The Black Scholar*, (May 1970): 43-50.

Giovanni, Nikki. *Blues For All The Changes*. New York: William Morrow and Company, Inc., 1999.

Haley, Alex; and Malcolm X. *The Autobiography of Malcolm X*. 1964; New York: Ballantine Books, 1993.

Handler, M.S. "Wilkins Says Black Power Leads Only to Black Death." *New York Times*, July 6, 1966: 1, 14.

Handler, M. S. "Whitney Young Urges Attempt Be Made to Reach Ghetto Unreachables." *New York Times*, August 1, 1966, 2.

Hampton, Henry; and Steve Fayer. *Voices of Freedom: An Oral History of the Civil Rights Movement*. New York: Bantam Books, 1990.

Halberstam, David. *The Children*. New York: Random House, 1998.

Havel, Vaclav. "The Power of the Powerless." In *Open Letters: Selected Writings 1965-1990*, edited by Paul Wilson, 125-214. New York: Vintage Books, 1990.

Heath, G. Louis, ed. *The Black Panther Leaders Speak: Huey P. Newton, Bobby Seale, Eldridge Cleaver and Company Speak Out Through the Black Panther Party's Official Newspaper_*. Metuchen: The Scarecrow Press, Inc., 1976.

Hill, Robert, and Barbara Bair. ed. *Marcus Garvey Life and Lessons*. Berkeley: University of California Press, 1987.

Hilliard, David. "What You Are Speak So Loud I Hardly Hear What You Say." *The Black Panther*, November 8, 1969, 4.

Hilliard, David. "If You Want Peace You've Got To Fight For It." *The Black Panther*, November 22, 1969, 3-4.

Hilliard, David. "The Ideology of the Black Panther Party." In Philip S. Foner, ed. *The*

Black Panthers Speak. 1970; New York: DA Capo Press, 1995.

Hoffman, Abbie. "Black Power: A Discussion." *Partisan Review* 35 (Spring 1968): 209-211.

Hooks, Bell. *Killing Rage: Ending Racism.* New York: Henry Holt & Company, Inc., 1995.

Howard, John R. "The Making of A Black Muslim." *Society* 35 (Jan/Feb 1998): 32 - 40.

Hughes, Langston, and Milton Meltzer, *et al,* ed. *A Pictorial History of Black Americans.* New York: Crown Publishers, Inc., 1956.

Hughes, Langston. *Selected Poems of Langston Hughes.* New York: Vintage Books, 1990.

Jessup, John K. "An Urgent New Reach to Be Equal." *Life,* June 3, 1966, 88-98.

Johnson, Thomas A. "Black Nationalists Gain More Attention in Harlem." *New York Times,* July 3, 1966, 1, 29.

King, Martin Luther, Jr. "Letter From A Birmingham Jail." In *A Testament of Hope: The Essential Writings of Dr. Martin Luther King, Jr.,* edited by James Washington, 289-300. New York: Harper Collins, 1986.

King, Martin Luther, Jr. *A Testament of Hope: The Essential Writings of Dr. Martin Luther King, Jr.,* edited by James Washington, 64-72. New York: Harper Collins, 1986.

King, Martin Luther, Jr. "Black Power Defined." In *A Testament of Hope: The Essential Writings of Dr. Martin Luther King, Jr.,* edited by James Washington, 303-312. New York: Harper Collins, 1986.

King, Martin Luther, Jr. "The Ethical Demands for Integration." *A Testament of Hope: The Essential Writings of Martin Luther King, Jr.,* 117-125. New York: Harper Collins, 1986.

King, Martin Luther, Jr. "Pilgrimage to Nonviolence." In *A Testament of Hope: The Essential Writings of Martin Luther King, Jr.,* edited by James Washington, 35-40. New York: Harper Collins, 1986.

King, Martin Luther, Jr. "Where Do We Go from Here." In *A Testament of Hope: The Essential Writings of Martin Luther King, Jr.,* edited by James Washington, 555-633. New York: Harper Collins, 1986.

King, Martin Luther, Jr. "Where Do We Go from Here: Chaos or Community." In James Washington, ed. *A Testament of Hope: The Essential Writings of Martin Luther King, Jr.* New York: Harper Collins, 1986.

King, Martin Luther, Jr. "A Testament of Hope." In *A Testament of Hope: The Essential Writings of Martin Luther King, Jr.,* edited by James Washington, 313-328. New York: Harper Collins, 1986.

King, Martin Luther, Jr. "I See the Promised Land." In *A Testament of Hope: The Essential Writings of Dr. Martin Luther King, Jr.,* edited by James Washington, 279-286. New York: Harper Collins, 1986.

Lester, Julius. "The Necessity For Separatism." *Ebony,* August, 1970, 167-169.

Levering Lewis, David. "Martin Luther King, Jr., And The Promise of Nonviolent Populism." In *Black Leaders of the Twentieth Century,* edited by John Hope Franklin and August Meier, 277-303. Urbana and Chicago: University of Illinois Press, 1982.

Lewis, John, and Michael D' Orso. *Walking With the Wind: A Memoir of the Movement.* New York: Simon and Schuster, 1998.

Lewis, John. Personal Interview. 28 Apr. 1998.

Lincoln, C. Eric. *The Black Muslims in America.* 3rd edition. Trenton: Africa World Press, Inc., 1994.

Ling, Peter. "Martin Luther King's Half-Forgotten Dream." *History Today,* April, 1998, 17 - 23.

Ling-Ling, Yeh. "Immigration Won't Work Without Assimilation." *Star Ledger,* May 23, 1999, Sec. 10: 3-6.

Little, Malcolm. "The Black Revolution." *Malcolm X Speaks,* edited by George Brietman, 140-145. New York: Merit Publishing & Betty Shabazz, 1965.

Little, Malcolm. "To Mississippi Youth." In *Malcolm X Speaks,* edited by George Brietman, 137-140. New York: Merit Publishing & Betty Shabazz, 1965.

Little, Malcolm. "The Ballot or the Bullet." In *Malcolm X Speaks,* edited by George Brietman, 20-46. New York: Merit Publishing & Betty Shabazz, 1965.

Little, Malcolm. "Malcolm X Founds the Organization of Afro-American Unity." In *Black Protest Thought in the Twentieth Century,* edited by August Meier et. Al., 2nd ed., 414-415. Indianapolis and New York: the Bobbs Merrill Company Inc., 1971.

Lynd, Staughton, "Introduction." *The New Left: A Collection of Essays,* edited by Pricilla Long, 1-5. Boston: Porter Sargeant Publishers, 1969.

Malveaux, Julianne. "Banking on US: The State of Black Wealth." *Essence,* October, 1998, 100 - 163.

Massey, Douglas S. and Nancy A. Denton. *American Apartheid: Segregation and the:Making of the Underclass.* Massachusetts: Harvard University Press, 1993.

Matusow, Allen J. *The Unraveling of America: A History of Liberalism in the 1960s.* New York: Harper & Row, 1986

Max, Steve. "The Mississippi Freedom Democratic Party: Background and Recent Development." The Records of the Mississippi Freedom Democratic Party (1964-1965) at the King Center.

McCartney, John T. *Black Power Ideologies: An Essay in African-American Political Thought.* Philadelphia: Temple University Press, 1992.

McKissick, Floyd B. "The Way to A Black Ideology." *The Black Scholar* (December: 1969) 14-17.

McKissick, Floyd B. "The Civil Rights Movement is Dead." *Notes of the Chairman-1966,* The Papers of the Congress of Racial Equality (1944-1968) at the King Center.

McKissick, Floyd B. "Constructive Militancy: A Philosophy and A Program." *Notes of the Chairman-1966,* The Papers of the Congress of Racial Equality (1944-1968) at the King Center.

McKissick, Floyd B. "What is Core Doing Now?" *The Corelator-1967,* The Papers of the Congress of Racial Equality (1944-1968) at the King Center.

McKissick, Floyd B. "A Black Manifesto." *Notes of the Chairman-1967,*The Papers of the Congress of Racial Equality (1944-1968) at the King Center.

McKissick, Floyd B. "Programs for Black Power." *Notes of the Chairmann-1967,* The Papers of the Congress of Racial Equality (1944-1968) at the King Center.

Meier, August, and Elliott Rudwick. *CORE : A Study in The Civil Rights Movement.* New York: Oxford University Press, 1973.

Meier, August; and John H. Bracey. "The NAACP As A Reform Movement, 1909-1965: To Reach the Conscience of America." LIX, No. 1 (February 1993): 3-30.

Monroe, Sylvester. "The Mirage of Farrakhan." *Newsweek,* October 30, 1995: 52.

Moses, Wilson Jeremiah. *The Golden Age of Black Nationalism, 1850-1925* Hamden: Archon Books, 1978.

Muhammad, Elijah. "From A Program for Self-Development." In *Modern Black Nationalism from Marcus Garvey to Louis Farrakhan,* edited by William L. Van Deburg, New York: New York University Press, 1997.

Muhammad, Elijah. "Know Thyself." In *Modern Black Nationalism from Marcus Garvey to Louis Farrakhan*, edited by William L. Van Deburg, 405-410. New York: New York University Press, 1997.

Muhammad, Elijah. "The Making of Devil." In *Modern Black Nationalism from Marcus Garvey to Louis Farrakhan*, edited by William L. Van Deburg, 395-400. New York: New York University Press, 1997.

NAACP. "NAACP 57th Annual Convention Resolutions." In the Records of the NAACP Part IV, at the Library of Congress, Washington, D.C., Box# A3, Folder 2.

Naison, Mark. *Communists in Harlem During the Depression*. Urbana: University of Illinois Press, 1983.

National Urban League. "Implementing A New Thrust." In the Records of the National Urban League Part III, at the Library of Congress, Washington, D. C., Box# 35, Folder 11.

National Committee of Negro Churchmen. "Black Power." *New York Times,* July 6, 1966: E5.

Newton, Huey P. "The Black Panthers." *The Black Panther,* August 23, 1969, 9-10.

Newton, Huey P. "In Defense of Self-Defense: Executive Mandate Number One." In *The Black Panthers Speak,* edited by Philip S. Foner, 40-41. 1970; New York: DA Capo Press, 1995.

Newton, Huey P. "The Correct Handling of a Revolution." In *The Black Panthers Speak*, edited by Philip S. Foner, 41-45. 1970; New York: DA Capo Press, 1995.

Newton, Huey P. "Functional Definition of Politics." In *The Black Panthers Speak*, edited by Philip S. Foner, 45-47. 1970; New York: DA Capo Press, 1995.

Newton, Huey P. "Huey Newton Talks to the Movement About the Black Panther Party, Cultural Nationalism, SNCC, Liberals and White Revolutionaries." In *The Black Panthers Speak*, edited by Philip S. Foner, 50-66. 1970; New York: DA Capo Press, 1995.

Newton, Huey P. "To the RNA." In *The Black Panthers Speak*, edited by Philip S. Foner, 70-73. 1970; New York: DA Capo Press, 1995.

Newton, Huey P. "On the Defection of Eldridge Cleaver From the Black Panther Party And the Defection of the Black Panther Party From the Black Community." In *The Black Panthers Speak,* edited by Philip S. Foner, 272-278. 1970; New York: DA Capo Press, 1995.

Newton, Huey P. *Revolutionary Suicide.* New York: Harcourt Brace Jovanovich, Inc., 1973.

Newton, Huey P. *To Die For the People: The Writings of Huey P Newton.* New York: Writers and Readers Publishing, Inc., 1973.

Ngozi-Brown, Scot. "The US Organization, Maulana Karenga, And Conflict With The Black Panther Party." *Journal of Black Studies* 28, (Nov. 1997): 157 - 171.

Oates, Stephen B. *Let the Trumpet Sound: A Life of Martin Luther King, Jr.* New York: Harper and Row, 1982.

Obadele, Imari Abubakari. "The Struggle Is For Land." *The Black Scholar* (February 1972): 24-35.

Obadele, Imari Abubakari. "National Black Elections Held by the Republic of New Africa." *The Black Scholar* (October 1975): 27-38.

Obadele, Imari Abubakari. "The Struggle of the Republic of New Africa." *The Black Scholar* (June 1974): 32-41

Ogunleye, Tolagbe. "Dr. Martin Robison Delany, 19th Century Africana Womanist: Reflections on His Avante-Garde Politics Concerning Gender, Colonialism, and Nation Building." *Journal of Black Studies* 28 (May 1998): 628 - 650.

O'Reilly, Kenneth. *Racial Matters: the FBI's Secret File on Black America (1960-1972).* New York: The Free Press, 1991.

Patterson, Orlando. "Going Separate Ways: The History of and Old Idea." *Newsweek,* October 30, 1995, 43.

Patton, John M. "I Have A Dream: The Performance of Theology with the Power of Orality." In *Martin Luther King, Jr. and the Sermonic Power of Public Discourse,* edited by Carolyn Calloway-Thomas, 200-210. Tuscaloosa and London: University of Alabama Press, 1993.

Pinkney, Alphonso. "The Assimilation of Afro-Americans." *The Black Scholar* (December 1969): 36-46.

Poussaint, Alvin F. "A Negro Psychiatrist Explains the Negro Psyche." *New York Times,* August 20, 1967, 52-80.

Poussaint, Alvin F. "How the White Problem Spawned Black Power." *Ebony,* August, 1967, 88-94.

Poussaint, Alvin F. "A Psychiatrist Looks At Black Power." *Ebony,* March, 1969: 142-152.

Randall, Dudley, ed. *The Black Poets.* New York: Bantam Books, 1971.

Reed, Roy. "Meredith Begins Mississippi Walk to Combat Fear." *New York Times,* June 6, 1966, 27.

Reed, Roy. "Meredith Regrets He Was Not Armed." *New York Times,* June 8, 1966: 1, 26.

Roberts, Gene. "Troopers Shove Group Resuming Meredith March." *New York Times,* June 8, 1966, 1, 26.

Roberts, Gene. "March's Leaders Demand Action by U.S. On Rights." *New York Times,* June 9, 1966, 1.

Roberts, Gene. "Why the Cry for Black Power." *New York Times,* July 4, 1966, 29.

Roberts, Gene. "Mississippi Reduces Police Protection for Marchers." *New York Times,* June 17, 1966, 1, 33.

Rogoff, Edward G., and John Trinkaus. "Perhaps the times Have Not Yet Caught Up to Marcus Garvey, An Early Champion of Ethnic Entrepreneurship." *Journal of Small Business Management* 36 (July 1998): 66 - 72.

Rustin, Bayard. "Black Power And Coalition Politics." *Down The Line: The Selected Writings of Bayard Rustin.* Chicago: Quadrangle Books, 1971. 154-165.

Sackett, Russell. "Plotting A War On Whitey: If Negro Leadership Fails, Extremists Are Set And Eager for Violence." Life, June 10, 1966, 100-112.

Seale, Bobby. *A Lonely Rage: The Autobiography of Bobby Seale.* New York: New York Times Books, 1978.

Sellers, Cleveland, and Robert Terrell. *The River of No Return: The Autobiography of A Black Militant and the life and Death of SNCC.* Jackson: University of Mississippi Press, 1973.

Shipp, E. R. "Little Rock Still a Hard Place." *Daily News,* September 26, 1997: 37.

Sitkoff, Harvard. *The Struggle For Black Equality.* New York: Hill & Wang, 1993.

Southern Christian Leadership Conference. "The Ultimate Aim is the Beloved Community." In August Meier, *et al,* ed. *Black Protest Thought in the Twentieth Century.* (2nd edition). Indianapolis and New York: The Bobbs-Merrill Company Inc., 1971. 302-306.

Student Nonviolent Coordinating Committee. "Position Paper on Black Power." In *Modern Black Nationalism: From Marcus Garvey to Louis Farrakhan,* edited by William L. Van De Burg, 120-122. New York: New York University Press, 1997.

Student Nonviolent Coordinating Committee. "We Must Fill Ourselves With Hate For

All White Things." In *Black Protest Thought in the Twentieth Century,* edited by August Meier, et. al., 315-320. 2nd ed. Indianapolis and New York: The Bobbs Merrill Company Inc., 1971.

Styles, Gloria. Personal Interview. July 10, 1998.

Tate, Gayle T. "Free Black Resistance In The Antebellum Era, 1830 to 1860." *Journal of Black Studies* 28, (July 1998): 764 - 783.

Tillman, James A. "The Riot Commission Report: 1968, A Negro Psychologist finds a Fatal Flaw." In *Chronicles of Negro Protest: A Background Book Documenting the History of Black Power,* edited by Bradford Chambers, 117-120. New York: Parents' Magazine Press, 1968.

Turner, James. "The Sociology of Black Nationalism." *The Black Scholar* (December 1969): 18-27.

Tyson, Timothy B. "Robert F. Williams, Black Power, and the Roots of the African American Freedom Struggle." *The Journal of American History* 85 (Sept. 1998): 540 - 570.

Van De Burg, William L. *New Day in Babylon: The Black Power Movement And American Culture.* Chicago and London: The University of Chicago Press, 1992.

Washington, Booker T. *Up From Slavery.* 1901; New York: Penguin Books, 1986.

Weisbrot, Robert. *Freedom Bound: A History of America's Civil Rights Movement.* New York: Plume, 1990.

Weiss, Nancy J. "Whitney M. Young, Jr.: Committing The Power Structure to the Cause Of Civil Rights." In *Black Leaders Of the Twentieth Century,* edited by John Hope Franklin and August Meier, 331-358. Urbana and Chicago: University of Illinois Press, 1982.

Wesley Johnson, James. "Kawaida And Kuminalism: Basis For A New African American Ecumenism. "*Journal of Religious Thought* 48 (Summer/Fall - 1991): 20 - 40.

Wells, Samuel. Personal Interview. July 10, 1998.

West, Cornel. *Race Matters.* New York: Vintage Books, 1993.

Wilkerson, Isabel. "Soul Survivor: From Stokely Carmichael to Kwame Ture, Still Ready for the Revolution." *Essence,* May 1998, 109 - 190.

Wilkins, Roy. "Separatists Forget That Their Siren Call has repeatedly Failed." *Ebony,* August, 1970, 54-60.

Wilkins, Roy. "For Shock Troops and Solid Moves." In *Black Protest Thought in the Twentieth Century,* edited by August Meier, et. al., 321. 2nd ed. Indianapolis and New York: The Bobbs Merrill Company Inc., 1971.

Wilkins, Roy. "Keynote Address of Roy Wilkins, Executive Director-National Association for the Advancement of Colored People before its Fifty Seventh Annual Convention." In the Roy Wilkins Papers, at the Library of Congress, Washington, D. C., Box # A3, Folder 6.

Wilkins, Roy. "The Disrupters." In the Roy Wilkins Papers, at the Library of Congress. Washington, D. C., Box # 39, Folder 5.

Wilkins, Roy. "SNCC's New Road." In the Roy Wilkins Papers, at the Library of Congress. Washington, D. C., Box# 39, Folder 5.

Wilkins, Roy. "The March in Retrospect." In the Roy Wilkins Papers, at the Library of Congress. Washington, D. C., Box# 39, Folder 5.

Wilkins, Roy. "Meredith's Successors." In the Roy Wilkins Papers, at the Library of Congress. Washington, D. C., Box# 39, Folder 5.

Wilkins, Roy. "The Riot Inciters." In the Roy Wilkins Papers, at the Library of Congress, Washington, D. C., Box# 39, Folder 5.

Wilkins, Roy. "Damage to Our Children." In the Roy Wilkins Papers, at the Library of

Congress. Washington, D. C. Box# 39, Folder 4.

Wilkins, Roy. "In Defense of the Middle Class." In the Roy Wilkins Papers, at the Library of Congress. Washington, D. C. Box# 37, Folder 3.

Wilkins, Roy. "Black Power and Jewish Defense League." In the Roy Wilkins Papers, at the Library of Congress. Washington, D. C. Box# 37, Folder 7.

Wilkins, Roy. "The Kind of Backbone We Now Need." In the Roy Wilkins Papers, at the Library of Congress. Washington, D. C. Box# 37, Folder 7.

Wilkins, Roy. "The Destructionists." In the Roy Wilkins Papers, at the Library of Congress, Washington, D. C., Box# 39, Folder 5.

Wilkins, Roy. "Remarks of Roy Wilkins Executive Director- National Association for The Advancement of Colored People Before its 58th Annual Convention." In the Records of the NAACP (Part IV), at the Library of Congress, Washington, D. C., Box# A5, Folder 4.

Wilkins, Roy. "Whither Black Power." *Crisis,* (August-September) 1966: 353 -355.

Wilkins, Roy. "What Now-One Negro Leaders Answer." In the Roy Wilkins Papers, at the Library of Congress, Washington, D. C., Box# 37, Folder 6.

Wilkins, Roy, and Tom Mathews. *Standing Fast: The Autobiography of Roy Wilkins.* 1982. New York: DA Capo Press, 1994.

Williams, Robert F. "For Effective Self Defense." In August Meier, et al, ed. *Black Protest Thought in the Twentieth Century.* 2nd ed. Indianapolis and New York: The Bobbs Merrill Company, Inc., 1971.

Young, Whitney M. "We Are Separated That's the Cause of All Our Woes." *Ebony,* August, 1970, 90-99.

Young, Whitney M. "For Protest Plus Corrective Measures." In *Black Protest Thought in the Twentieth Century,* edited by August Meier, et. al., 320-324. 2nd ed. Indianapolis and New York: The Bobbs Merrill Company, Inc., 1971.

Young, Whitney M. "To Fulfill These Rights." In the Records of the National Urban League Part III, at the Library of Congress, Washington, D. C., Box# 48, Folder 44.

Young, Whitney M. "To Integrate Hope." In the Records of the National Urban League Part II, at the Library of Congress, Washington, D. C., Box# 48, Folder 39.

Zepp, Ira G. *The Social Vision of Martin Luther King, Jr.* New York: Carlson Publishing, Inc., 1989.

Unsigned Articles

"At the Breaking Point." *Time,* July 15, 1966, 15-16.

"Background on the Development of Political Strategy and Political Education in Lowndes County, Alabama." *Community Relations-1966, Alabama,* The Student Nonviolent Coordinating Committee Records (1959-1972) at the King Center.

"Black Power Defined." *Public Relations Files-1966,* The Papers of the Congress of Racial Equality (1944-1968) at the King Center.

"Black Power: Road to Disaster." *Newsweek,* August 22, 1966, 32-57.

"Black Power Must Be Defined." *Life,* July 22, 1966, 4.

"Civil Rights." *New York Times,* February 12, 1965, 16-17.

"Core Will Insist On Black Power." *New York Times,* July 4, 1966, 16.

"Crisis and Commitment." *Crisis* (November 1966): 474-477.

"Dr. King Receives $100,000 Donation." *New York Times,* July 6, 1966, 15.

"Excerpts From Paper On Which the Black Power Philosophy is Based." *New York*

Times, August 5, 1966, 10.

"How Can People Work Together in A Political Organization?" *Community Relations-1965, Alabama,* The Student Nonviolent Coordinating Committee Records (1959-1972) at the King Center.

"Is This The Party You Want?" *Political Campaign Poster Lowndes County, Alabama-1965,* The Student Nonviolent Coordinating Committee Records (1959-1972) at the King Center.

"L.A. Chapter Opens Bunchy Carter Free Health Clinic." *The Black Panther,* December 11, 1969.

"NAACP Annual Meeting." *Crisis* (January-February) 1967: 11-17.

"The Necessity For Southern Urban Organizing." The SNCC Papers at the State Historical Society of Wisconsin.

"The New Negro Mood." *Life,* June 10, 1966, 4.

"The New Racism." *Time,* July 1, 1966, 11-13.

"Prospectus For An Atlanta Project." The SNCC Papers at the State Historical Society of Wisconsin.

"Oakland Boycott." *The Black Panther,* June 10, 1968.

"Rules of the Black Panther Party." *The Black Panther,* November 16, 1968.

"Urban League Chief Deplores the Fight Over Black Power." *New York Times,* August 5, 1966, 10.

"Vote Nov 8th!" *Lowndes County Campaign Poster-1965,* The Student Nonviolent Coordinating Committee Records (1959-1972) at the King Center.

"What We Want What We Believe: Black Panther Party Platform and Program." *The Black Panther ,* November 16, 1968.

INDEX

About the Author

Hettie V. Williams received a BA degree in history from Rowan University located in Glassboro, New Jersey in 1994 and a graduate degree in history from Monmouth University located in West Long Branch, New Jersey with a concentration in African American history in 2000. Her research interests include topics in recent American history, African American history, the African Diaspora, along with identity and race theory. She has contributed biographical entries and thematic essays to such collections as the *Encyclopedia of the Gilded Age and Progressive Era* and the *Encyclopedia of African American History*. She has taught courses on the history of African Americans, the history of the United States, World Civilizations, and interdisciplinary studies at various institutions. Her current research includes a forthcoming work entitled *There is Confusion: Black Identity in the African Diaspora.* Currently, she is a Lecturer in African American History in the Department of History and Anthropology at Monmouth University.